Praise

"Kathleen has a knack for gathering souls in the shelter of common stories, simple answers, and loving support–the things we mothers always need and yet so seldom ask for. I have been a grateful guest in Kathleen's home. Now, in this book, you can be her guest too. Invite yourself in to a well-crafted life."

Karen Maezen Miller,
author of *Momma Zen, Hand Wash Cold* and *Paradise in Plain Sight*

"Kathleen Ann Harper weaves poignant stories from her experience as a mother of young children into a book that will mesmerize and inspire you. *The Well-Crafted Mom* takes us beyond artfully written vignettes on the challenges of motherhood and reveals great ideas, practical tools, and easy mind shifts that can change a frenzied mom's life. The fun and meaningful craft projects at the end of every chapter are like balm for a stressed out spirit. This is a unique and powerful book every mother should read."

Jill Farmer,
author of *There's Not Enough Time... and Other Lies We Tell Ourselves*

"A part of every mother I know is in this book. I laughed and I cried like I would having an honest conversation with a good friend. Harper reminds us we are not alone on this journey of modern motherhood and, like a good friend does, Harper guides the reader through that tunnel to discover the light at the other end. Along the way are thoughtful soul-nourishing craft ideas that provide something often not found in western culture: ritual, as a symbolic marker for each transition. Written with exceptional honesty, and with each point so well cited, *The Well-Crafted Mom* weaves the past, present, and future of motherhood into an inspiring, encouraging, and hopeful path that every mother deserves."

Suzanne P. Reese, IAIMT,
author of *Baby Massage: Soothing Strokes for Healthy Growth,*
and singer/songwriter of *Talk to Me: Happy Tunes for Healthy Growth*

"A shot in the arm of inspiration, Kathleen Ann Harper's *The Well-Crafted Mom* will help you feel so much more capable of holding onto your soul in the midst of relentless day-to-day parenting. A spiritual tune-up, this practical guide and the craft projects that end each chapter provide calming antidotes to the stress that often accompanies motherhood. This book is a beautiful resource for any mom."

Elisa Fisher, Director of The Ultimate Women's Expo

"They say parenting doesn't come with an instruction manual. Well now, it does! *The Well-Crafted Mom* is an empowering guide to better parenting, explained by a true master of nurturing creative and vibrant families. Amidst a field of parenting experts, Kathleen Ann Harper shines."

Evan Zislis,
author of *ClutterFree Revolution: Simplify Your Stuff,
Organize Your Life & Save the World*

the Well- Crafted MOM

A Do-It-Yourself Guide for Making a Life You Love

Kathleen Ann Harper

NEW YORK

LONDON • NASHVILLE • MELBOURNE • VANCOUVER

The Well-Crafted Mom

A Do-It-Yourself Guide for Making a Life You Love

Published in New York, New York, by Morgan James Publishing. Morgan James is a trademark of Morgan James, LLC. www.MorganJamesPublishing.com

The Morgan James Speakers Group can bring authors to your live event. For more information or to book an event visit The Morgan James Speakers Group at www.TheMorganJamesSpeakersGroup.com.

ISBN 9781683508267 paperback
ISBN 9781683508274 eBook
Library of Congress Control Number: 2017916966

Cover Design by:
Rachel Lopez

Interior Design by:
Paul Curtis

In an effort to support local communities, raise awareness and funds, Morgan James Publishing donates a percentage of all book sales for the life of each book to Habitat for Humanity Peninsula and Greater Williamsburg.

Get involved today! Visit
www.MorganJamesBuilds.com

For my husband and children,
who helped me craft my wings.

Table of Contents

Introduction

*"The craft of questions, the craft of stories, the craft of the hands–
all these are the making of something, and that something is soul."*
Clarissa Pinkola Estés

Having a baby can be like being thrown into the deep end of the ocean. Some mothers do fine. They figure out how to dog paddle to shore, or maybe they have family and friends who throw lifelines, pulling them to safety. You may have a strong support system in place, like relatives who live nearby and a network of close friends, or you may have paid assistance, like a nanny or sleep consultant who helps you to stay afloat.

Or maybe motherhood is a daily struggle of trying to keep your head above water.

That's what motherhood used to be like for me. I had wanted children for years, but was waiting for the right man, the right time. Before I had kids, I was so sure I would be the very best mom. And after my two boys came–although there were moments when I could see I was doing okay as a parent–most of the time I felt like a failure. I saw other moms at the co-op preschool, in the grocery store, at the park, and they looked happy, well-rested, showered. What was I missing?

In my professional career, I had managed a busy Starbucks store, coordinated special events for the San Francisco Zoo, managed a human resources department for a medium-sized company, and built my own massage therapy business. Why was managing two small children and a household so much harder? I heard "it will get better" from my friends and family, even from strangers, but I didn't want to wait for my kids to be older, out of diapers, and all the way in elementary school to start enjoying motherhood more completely.

There's a time for many moms when they come up for air. The timing depends on what kind of child you have (temperamental or mellow), how many children you care for, how much support is available to you, the ages of your children, and how well you cope with chaos and change.

My mom came up for air when I was 12 and she decided (with six kids between the ages of four and 14) to go back to college, where she finished her undergraduate degree and then earned a master's degree in public health. For me, it was when my youngest was 18 months old and I felt like I was unraveling, like something precious was being pulled from me every day, strand by strand. I knew that if I didn't take steps to make my life different, there wouldn't be anything left for me to give.

I went to parenting workshops, read a mountain of books, and saw a couples counselor with my husband to mend my marriage when my unravelling threatened to pull apart the loose threads of our relationship. During the early years of motherhood, I felt like I was reweaving the fabric of me, using whatever I could find to repair the holes, to feel whole and mended. It was a slow, patchwork process, but I eventually developed tools to feel more capable, calm, and confident.

"The only stability is our trust in the process and our intuitive awareness that Love's very nature is to consume and call us home," writes Sera Beak in *Red, Hot and Holy.*

I found my way home and, once there, I was able to see so many other mothers adrift. I studied to become a certified life coach to help moms, not only with tools and ideas to make day-to-day problems more manageable, but by creating a community of support and providing a wealth of resources, a life raft for moms who want to find a way to their own safe shore.

This book is organized into three sections–Rest, Craft, and Fly–based on how I work with moms in my one-on-one sessions and in my group programs. *Rest* helps you to build a solid foundation so that you can *craft* the life that you truly want, which gives you more time, stamina, and momentum to *fly* toward what sustains you.

Each chapter begins with a story that represents a turning point for me, a lesson I needed to learn. Included in each chapter is theoretical and practical information from thought leaders, authors, and healers to help you create new ways to approach motherhood.

At the end of each chapter is a Coaching + Craft project–a practical craft idea taken from my monthly community gatherings for moms. During their time at the craft table, moms can create without interruption (a novel activity for many moms with small children). The craft project gives moms the opportunity to integrate the chapter's left-brain topic with a right-brain craft project, fusing logical concepts with artistic expression, connecting practical ideas with fanciful fun.

The Coaching + Craft projects at the end of each chapter are meant to be simple ways for you to make meaningful mementos to remind you of the small but mighty steps you can take to carve out more time for yourself, feel better about your parenting, and figure out what comes next.

"The answers I have found–through considering the work of my own hands, through the practical education of a life in craft, and through the shared experiences of others–all seem to lead back to one fundamental truth: we practice contemporary craft as a process of self-transformation," writes Peter Korn in *Why We Make Things and Why It Matters*. This was certainly true for me. When I returned to making jewelry, creating collages, and writing in my journal after my children were born, I rediscovered a wealth of healing that existed nowhere else in my life. Once I carved out the time for creativity, I uncovered a deep well of patience, an ocean of happiness, and endless love to spread around.

Motherhood hones who you are. As you lean into life's rough edges, you become more adept with using your greatest gifts. "The difference between happy people and unhappy ones is that happy people have found a use for themselves, like a good tool," writes author Barbara Kingsolver. I hope this book helps you to become as skilled as any master artisan, creating a fulfilling life for yourself and your family that is as beautiful and redemptive as a well-crafted work of art.

Part 1

REST

Room
Expect Less
Say No to the Book Fair
Take Your Time

"What is really hard, and really amazing, is giving up on being perfect and beginning the work of becoming yourself."

Anna Quindlen

Chapter One

Room

"We think that the point is to pass the test or overcome the problem, but the truth is that things don't really get solved. They come together and they fall apart. Then they come together again and fall apart again. It's just like that. The healing comes from letting there be room for all of this to happen: room for grief, for relief, for misery, for joy."
Pema Chodron

I'm too selfish to be a mom, I realized at 3:30 one morning, while breastfeeding my younger son in the dark. I had lived alone for too long in my 20s and 30s. I didn't get married until way too late in my life. I had always been able to leave relationships too easily when things got hard.

My second son was a fussy baby, so after feeding him from one breast, I had to put him high on my shoulder and pat his back for ten minutes until he finally burped, feed him on the other breast, and wait until he burped again. Then I would hold him upright for at least another ten minutes before laying him down next to me in bed. Any variation from the routine and he'd cry inconsolably, high-pitched and almost angry, his knees toward his chest, red-faced and sweaty.

I was already pretty sure I was failing as a mom, so I followed the feeding, burping, holding procedure religiously, not wanting to add more evidence to what was already a deep file of my shortcomings. But I could list yesterday's transgressions in my head and I reviewed them in the dark while I waited for the burp: yelled at my older son because he made a huge wet mess in bathroom, didn't smile back at the baby, only half-listened to my son when he was telling me about his favorite part of preschool, hoped that the baby couldn't understand English when I cried on the phone with my best friend and listed all the reasons why it was a mistake to have a second child.

How did my life get to this point? All my life, I succeeded at everything I directed my attention to—education, my career, building my own busy massage therapy practice after becoming disillusioned with the corporate world. My mantra of *work hard, work harder* had never let me down.

Until now.

No matter how hard I worked, the unpredictability of my life with children created chaos for me. I used to be so organized and orderly. I lived alone for years, choosing small apartments with tiny kitchens and enjoyed finding the perfect places for my clothes in the closet, dishes in the cabinets, items on the shelves. There was a calm ease that came from knowing that everything had a place. I didn't get married until my late 30s and had my boys when I was 38 and 40; I'd had a deliciously long time to have things just right.

I thought I'd still be able to have things just right after my boys were born. I imagined the colorful baskets for toys, the changing table with drawers and shelves for supplies, the mesh plastic containers for the dishwasher to hold the accouterments for the bottles and breast pump accessories. And, as organized as I was with the house, I would be just as organized as a mom—as attuned to my child's schedule as I was to my own, meticulously finding the answers to all that I didn't know, mothering my children in a thoroughly researched way so my securely attached kids slept through the night, self-soothed, and practically potty trained themselves.

I had always wanted children but now that they were here, my beliefs about what a "good mom" looked like didn't match how I wanted to manage my time, raise my children, and be in my marriage. I resented how my relationship with my husband shifted into both of us taking more traditional, stereotypical roles. I believed that to be a good mom I should spend the majority of my time with my kids, put my children's needs before my own, and appreciate each and every experience of motherhood. A question I kept hearing was, "How do you enjoy being a mom?" as if there was no other option but to embrace and enjoy it all.

I wanted it back, that old life of mine. The organized, easy one. The life that felt so full of all that I chose, the riches I didn't even realize were treasures until now: sleep, that gorgeous, uninterrupted sleep from my single life; all the free time to squander and fritter away; the ability to make spontaneous choices of what to do in the moment. *Do I feel like reading or watching a movie? Should I go shopping now or tomorrow morning?* I wanted to open that treasure chest and run my hands through the bright opulence and enjoy the luxury of choice again.

My son burped and I shifted him so he was resting against my chest as I leaned back against the pillows. Ten more minutes of keeping him mostly upright, then carefully easing him onto the bed next to me, and then I could sleep.

My almost asleep-son took a quiet, feathery breath in the dark and I mentally kicked myself for being ungrateful. I had a good life, a loving and patient husband, beautiful healthy kids. I had no right to be unhappy. But I was.

"We must be willing to let go of the life we planned so as to have the life that is waiting for us," wrote Joseph Campbell, author of *The Hero with a Thousand Faces*. But the life I was living now, and the one waiting for me, were filled with all the ways I was failing. I should be able to get in and out of the grocery store without one of my children screaming, crying, or refusing to "bend in the middle" when I tried to lower him into the shopping cart seat. I shouldn't have to rewash laundry because I kept forgetting to move the clothes from the washer to the dryer. I should be able to keep my home from being an embarrassing disaster. I should be able to put together at least one meal a day when my husband, kids, and I were all sitting at the table together. Instead, we sat at the table in shifts and what we ate was like an afterthought, thrown together at the last minute. I served a lot of pasta.

At least in the organized, easy life that I had planned for myself, I was the perfect mom.

The Mean Manager

Seventy-five percent of mothers say that the stress they put on themselves to be "perfect" is much greater than any stress they feel from being judged by other moms. In another study, 64 percent of moms stated that parenting is more competitive now than it was in the past, with three-quarters of the moms surveyed agreeing that it's important to try to be a "perfect" mom. And when moms fail, they feel shame and fear that others will find out they're having trouble dealing with the challenges of being a parent.

What I've realized in my work as a life coach with moms is that all moms feel like they're failing at one point or another. Not spending enough time with your kids. Being distracted when spending time with your kids. Not enjoying the time that you spend with your kids. It's normal. What hurts is when perfectionism keeps you isolated and lonely, when it prevents you from being satisfied with how much you can do and accepting of what the day brings.

When my sons were young, I started noticing the voice in my head that I called the Mean Manager: hypercritical, holding exceptionally high standards for myself and my family, stuck in a compare-and-despair mindset. I realized that I could shift instead to thinking like what I imagined the kind caretaker of a fixer upper would say. "There's a bit of dust," the Kind Caretaker would say as she lovingly ran her finger along the dirty chair rail, "But the house has good bones." "The hardwood floors are a bit scratched here and there but the foundation is solid." I certainly wasn't the mommy equivalent of the Hearst Castle, but I realized there was a lot of ground between striving to be an impeccable mansion and feeling like a run-down shack. I wanted to make room for acceptance. I wasn't perfect but I wasn't a failure either.

So I did with my perfectionism what one mom had recommended I do with the overwhelming flood of toys. This mom of six children would separate her children's toys in big plastic bins from Target, leave one bin of toys in the house for the kids to play with, and store the other bins in the garage, high on a shelf. After three weeks, the old toys would be boxed up and taken to the garage and another batch of toys would come in to play.

In the same way, I could manage my perfectionist tendencies, one or two projects at a time. If I tried to do too much, my inner emotional home would be full of tools and building materials, completely torn-up and unlivable. I needed to take one small step, followed by another small step. So I focused on developing systems for the clean-up crew (my toddler and I) and then, in a few weeks, I created a plan for managing mealtime. I designated one day for doing the laundry–and set a timer so I remembered to transfer the wet clothes into the dryer. And when I messed up and forgot to bring the groceries in from the car because the baby had fallen asleep and the toddler and I had made a game of *how quiet can we be* as we crept into the house with the sleeping baby in the car seat, the Kind Caretaker just smiled and said, "Curb appeal. This house has great curb appeal."

Practical Advice – How to Harness Your Superpowers

Your brain is an evidence-making machine. When you have a thought, whether it's positive or negative, your brain starts searching for evidence to support it. If you tell yourself you're not doing enough for your kids or you're a bad mom or you're lazy, you can probably rattle off a long list of the many ways your thought is true.

The stories that you tell yourself about your life end up creating your life. This background noise in your mind can keep you in the pit of despair, in the same room with resentment, and holding hands with unhappiness.

When you change your story, however, you change your world, one little bit at a time. When you reframe your stories to turn yourself into a heroine who overcomes daily challenges rather than being burdened by them, your brain begins to recognize the truth–you are a superhero.

A daily homework assignment can create more powerful and positive feelings in your life. At least once a day, complete this sentence: "Today, I was a superhero because …"

Find a time that you can answer this question regularly. You can add it to your bedtime routine, like right after you've brushed your teeth, or you could answer the question when you're in a mid-afternoon slump and it seems like the day will never end. You could also make the question part of dinnertime with your family, giving everyone a chance to talk about their superhero moment of the day.

Here are some examples from everyday superheroes:

Today, I was a superhero because …

- I managed to prepare dinner even with an unhappy three-year-old hanging onto my ankles.
- I fought my way through rush hour traffic without losing my cool, even when an idiot cut me off and nearly caused an accident.
- I mastered a shopping trip to Costco (with kids in tow), loaded and unloaded the car singlehandedly, and put nearly everything away in the span of one afternoon.

Let this be your superpower: changing your life, one story at a time.

Coaching + Craft – Finding Joy Basket

This chapter's Coaching + Craft project is about discovering the joyful moments that happen every day. Paying attention to what brings you happiness is a small but mighty practice. "The thoughts we choose to think are the tools we use to paint the canvas of our lives," wrote Louise L. Hay. When you regularly pay attention to what brings you happiness you see and feel more goodness every day.

The Coaching + Craft projects in this book are powerful antidotes to unhappiness. As you link an art project to a fledging idea that you want to nurture, you build new thought patterns in your brain. Your finished creation acts as a reminder–especially if the craft project is something you see or use regularly–that deepens a new path of possibilities and strengthens the likelihood that you'll begin and maintain desired changes in how you think, feel and behave.

Coaching + Craft Project Supplies:

- A small- to medium-sized bowl to use as a mold for your joy basket
- A medium-sized bowl to hold the glue mixture
- Baking sheet
- Plastic wrap
- Medium weight yarn
- School glue
- Water
- Scissors
- Notepad
- Pen or pencil

Protect your work surface by covering it with newspaper or a plastic tablecloth. Wrap the small- to medium-sized bowl in plastic wrap, making sure to cover the rim of the bowl. Tuck the excess plastic wrap into the center of the bowl.

Place plastic wrap on the baking sheet to protect the surface and put the wrapped bowl upside down on the baking sheet.

Cut the yarn into approximately 20 strands, each about 24 inches in length.

In the medium-sized bowl, mix a half a cup of glue with a quarter of a cup of water. Soak the yarn in the glue mixture.

Using one strand of yarn at a time, wrap the outside of the plastic-wrapped bowl with the yarn, making sure to have the strands touch in as many places as possible. The more places the yarn touches, the stronger your basket will be.

When finished, let your basket dry for 72 hours. When your basket is completely dry, gently pull the yarn basket away from the plastic wrapped bowl. Use small scissors to cut away any dried pieces of glue remaining on your basket.

Put your joy basket in a high traffic location of your home or office. A good place might be your kitchen, stairs, or your desk. Place a small notepad and pen or pencil near or inside your joy bowl. Then, whenever you notice happy feelings, write down the activity, memory, or thought that created the joyful experience and put the note in the basket.

If you're not near your basket when a bit of everyday joy arises, make sure to make a note about your happy experience either in a notepad or in an app on your phone so you can add the moment to your joy basket later. It's important to keep track of your happiness as you go through your day. Your mind's built-in negativity bias means that it's very easy to forget the tiny, delicious joys that happen throughout your day.

Do the Joy Basket activity for at least a week, preferably for a longer period of time.

After your Joy Basket experiment is over, review your notes. Notice trends, like you're happiest when you're outdoors, spending time with a particular person, or engaged in a specific hobby or activity. Then, make plans to spend more time doing what fills your life with joy.

To see Joy Baskets made by moms in The Well-Crafted Mom's groups, visit thewellcraftedmom.com/coaching-craft.

Chapter Two

Expect Less

"That was the thing about the world: it wasn't that things were harder than you thought they were going to be, it was that they were hard in ways that you didn't expect."
Lev Grossman

It had been an unrelenting day. The baby had a cold and trying to hold him still while using the bulb syringe to ease the snot out of his nose was like wrestling with a slippery baby hippo. If I didn't know better, I would swear that my son could close his nostrils at will. Because he was sick, he hadn't napped and had wanted to be held all day. When I put him in his swing so I had two free hands to make lunch for his brother, go to the bathroom, or blow my own nose, he wailed. My older son, seeing that his younger brother was monopolizing my attention, grew more demanding, "Read to me, Mommy," he said, poking a hardback book against my leg as I stood in the kitchen attempting to prepare dinner, the baby strapped against me in the Bjorn carrier. "Let's wait until after dinner and then we'll read three stories," I said in that falsely bright, it-will-all-be-okay tone of voice. But I had been asking my older boy to wait and wait all day. He had reached the end of his allotment of three-year-old patience and he fell apart in a messy tantrum at my feet.

I picked up my older son and awkwardly balanced him on my hip, his legs around the baby in the carrier. With boys crying, I walked to the foot of the stairs. "Hey, honey?" I called up to my husband, hard at work building his new business at his desk upstairs in the bay window of the master bedroom. "Could you come down to help?" I had spent all day pretending he wasn't home, reminding myself he was working just as if he was at a desk at an office somewhere miles away. I hated asking for backup–I knew how stressed he was about making up the lost income from a few accounts that had folded, and how hard he was working to provide for our family financially–but I felt sucked dry; there was nothing left to give.

"I'm in the middle of something," he answered. "I can't."

We argued, got through it, and then got through the many arguments that followed, and now we're enjoying some well-earned smooth sailing in our marriage. Going into parenthood, I believed my husband and I shared the same expectations of what co-parenting looked like–an all-hands-on-deck-in-a-storm sort of ideal. And, for the most part, it was true. My husband did help out with diaper changes, feedings, clean up, and household chores. He even took over the nighttime duties with the two boys when I fell apart after years of interrupted sleep. But even the term "help out" put his contribution in a different category than mine. I had expected him to be an equal participant, but in those early days, I was the captain. It was my job to run the ship and keep it on course, but I couldn't keep us afloat.

What to Expect

There's been a shift over the last several decades in how much moms expect from their partners in regard to parenting responsibilities and how much dads willingly provide. However, many moms still describe their husbands' contributions to childcare and household responsibilities in terms like "helping out" and "being supported by." This is what is commonly referred to as the "motherhood mandate"–the expectation that the father first provides for the family financially and then helps with childcare and household responsibilities with whatever time and energy is left over. Mothers, including moms who are employed full-time outside the home, are often expected to also provide selfless, undivided focus to their children and to all that parenting entails.

A study conducted by *ForbesWoman* and thebump.com found that 70 percent of all working mothers and 68 percent of stay-at-home moms felt resentful toward their partners, stemming from the overwhelming responsibilities of parenting and household chores. Mothers felt resentment for the unevenness of the division of labor, even when they preferred to do the chores themselves (because it's often easier to just do what needs to be done instead of explaining and then running the risk of having to redo what was done incorrectly). Two out of three moms said they felt like single parents because they handled all the household chores. Of the 1,200 women surveyed in the study, around 84 percent of stay-at-home moms said they didn't get a break from parenting even after their partner came home from work, despite the fact that nearly all respondents said they needed an occasional respite from being a mom. In fact, a full 50 percent of stay-at-home moms said they never had down time from parenting, while 96 percent said their partners did.

I lived with resentment like this for years. It encased my marriage and is what eventually drove my husband and me into much-needed couples counseling. Resentment is a giant clue that you're burning out. But when you don't get the needed break from the kids and can expect your spouse to only help out and not take over, how do you keep from working yourself down to nothing more than embers?

It turns out that how you perceive the stress in your life is far more important than the actual events you face day in and day out. "When you change the way you look at things, the things you look at change," said author and speaker Wayne Dyer. And the quickest way to change things for the better is to take a look at your expectations.

An old but often-cited study from 1992 by Australian nurse Carol McVeigh looked at the expectations of new mothers a year after giving birth. The higher the expectations a mom had going into motherhood about what parenting was going to be like–and the greater her anticipation of how much support she would experience from her spouse, friends and family–the deeper the disappointment she experienced in the year after giving birth, regardless of her actual circumstances. These inflated expectations can negatively influence not only a mom's relationship with her inner support circle, but her feelings of confidence in her parenting, as well. This study described the "Conspiracy of Silence" which isolates women from the harsh reality of what it's really like to care for an infant: exhausting, never-ending, and unrelenting.

After watching my close friend struggle with her two active boys who are about ten years older than mine, I knew how challenging mothering two boys could be. And the proliferation of mommy blogs with such article titles as "Ten Times You Wish You Had a Mute Button for Your Toddler," and "What I Wish I'd Known as a Newborn Mom," has broken any conspiracy of silence that remained. Blogs like Scary Mommy, Guerrilla Mom, and Renegade Mothering spill all of motherhood's dirty secrets for the world to see, from the fact that many moms have recurring thoughts of making a run for it the next time there's another moderately responsible grown-up in the house, to resentment toward spouse and children that rises and falls like a barometer of a mother's moods.

I saw firsthand how the most organized and patient women I knew believed they weren't succeeding as parents. Although in conversations with my friends before I became a mom, I reassured them that they were doing a great job, I secretly judged them for not trying hard enough. I knew I was stronger, smarter, and more determined, and had waited way too long for motherhood for it to be a massive, disappointing failure.

And then I became a mom.

I thought I would enjoy motherhood more. I thought the rewards for being sleepless, selfless, and steadfast for endless stretches of time would be greater than a few sloppy, wet kisses from my toddler. I loved those kisses, but the equation of effort versus enjoyment didn't balance. And what was tipping the scales in the negative direction was my expectations of what motherhood was supposed to be.

There's a comfort to expectations–they line up your day in an orderly fashion and act as a mental checklist of what you think is going to happen. The problem is that when the repairman doesn't arrive between 8:00 and noon, your child doesn't nap at 2:30, and your mom doesn't show up when she said she might, you're disappointed. Expectations also shadow your self-evaluation at the end of the day of what did or didn't get done. A survey by today.com and Insight Express showed that the average stress for moms is 8.5 on a scale of one to ten and 60 percent of mothers stated that their biggest cause of stress is not having enough time to get everything done. But who decides what goes into that bag of "everything that needs to get done?" You do, and it's based on your expectations.

Rakesh Sarin and Manel Baucells, economists and authors of the book *Engineering Happiness: A New Approach for Building a Joyful Life*, theorize that happiness equals reality minus expectations. But if you were to drop your expectations, to let them go like flotsam and jetsam on the sea of your experience, wouldn't happiness simply equal reality? And if you stop arguing with reality, would you be left with only happiness? "We can know that reality is good just as it is, because when we argue with it, we experience tension and frustration. We don't feel natural or balanced," writes Byron Katie in her book *Loving What Is: Four Questions That Can Change Your Life.* "When we stop opposing reality, action becomes simple, fluid, kind, and fearless."

Letting go of my expectations, and not arguing with reality, meant that I stopped evaluating my days with the parameters of good and bad, easy and hard, willing to stay or ready to run. It meant recognizing that my expectations were like Harry Potter's early efforts with casting the *Expecto Patronum* spell–I was attempting complicated magic meant to keep the darkness at bay but producing only a wispy wish for things to be different. As Karen Maezen Miller, author of *Momma Zen*, a book that lived on my bedside table for years, writes, "It's not a matter of expecting less or expecting more, expecting the best or expecting the worst. Expecting anything just gets in the way of the experience itself. And the experience itself is a stunner."

Practical Advice – A Recipe for Hope

In my personal dictionary, there's a difference between hope and expectation. Hope is a clean wish for the future. Hope is uplifting. Hope is given wings by your desires.

Expectations, on the other hand, are your perceptions of how other people should behave. They're not agreements–the arrangements you've made with others to balance the workload, handle priorities, and take care of the details–they're hopes burdened by duty and obligation, weighted by factors far out of your control, like rocks in your pocket when you're wishing for wings.

"Peace begins when expectation ends," wrote spiritual leader Sri Chinmoy in *The Wings of Joy: Finding Your Path to Inner Peace.*

Here's a recipe for turning expectations back to hope, shifting expectations into agreements, and creating more peace in the process:

Know your ingredients. To adjust your expectations, you'll want to know what they are. Make a list of your expectations, like what you expect your husband to do when he gets home from work, how you expect your children to behave at the playground, or when you expect your mom to help with babysitting. Your list can also include hopes for yourself that are tainted by your negative thoughts.

Come clean. Expectations are like dirty produce that's fresh from the farmer's market; they're hope covered in a layer of dirt that you'll want to wash away. Finding the hope underneath your expectations means coming clean and taking responsibility for your thoughts about what you think should happen.

It's often easier to blame other people for unmet expectations. "We blame when we're uncomfortable and experience pain—when we're vulnerable, angry, hurt, in shame, grieving," writes Brené Brown in *Daring Greatly*. "There's nothing productive about blame, and it often involves shaming someone or just being mean."

Rewriting your expectations can end the blame game. At my sons' elementary school, they call these adjusted phrases *I messages*. For example, "He should spend more time with me" becomes "I want him to spend more time with me." When you change your language to own your feelings without blame, you can see the hope that's been covered by a heavy layer of expectations.

You might discover other feelings when you wash away your expectations, like hurt, loneliness, or disappointment. If you do, handle them the same way—acknowledge them, revise them into an *I message*, and move on to the next step.

Cooking for one or two? Often, easing the discomfort created by expectations can be handled by coming clean. But when you uncover sadness, anger, or frustration, you'll want do a little more work. "I want my spouse to spend more time with me" might reveal disappointment that you don't have a passion as consuming as the one that has shifted his extra time and energy away from you. If this happens, figure out if your problem is a *me* or a *we*: can you resolve this issue on your own, by finding time to fulfill your own desires or spending time with friends, or does this issue need communication between you and your spouse for resolution? If it's a *we* issue, remember to use *I messages* to be kind, not accusatory, and to focus your communication on how you're feeling to reduce defensiveness and conflict.

Only one cook in the kitchen. Many times, it's not the expectations moms have for others but the expectations moms have for themselves that dirty up hope the most. Write down the expectations you have for yourself and notice where you use words like *supposed to, have to,* or *should.* These words are like pesticide–toxic obligations that cling to your hope, turning it into poisonous resentment if you're not careful. To wash the obligations from your hope, substitute *can, want, choose to,* or *will* for the dirty words, like this:

> *I have to complete these chores* becomes *I choose to complete these chores.*
> *I should be more patient* turns into *I will be more patient.*
> *I'm supposed to be happy* is cleaner when you say *I want to be happy.*

Cleaning up your self-talk may seem silly or inconsequential, but it's a shortcut for more happiness, hope, compassion, and peace. "For when we stray from peace and from the truth of things as they are, it is often because we have been busy turning one thing into another in our minds and hearts," writes Mark Nepo in *The Exquisite Risk: Daring to Live an Authentic Life.*

Coaching + Craft – Choose What You Carry

You expect that your husband will be home in time for you to take a break before starting the bedtime routine. You expect your mom will come and help after the new baby is born. You expect your toddler to have another good day at preschool, just like yesterday. Each expectation gets added to the bag you carry that's already full of what you expect from yourself in all your roles–parent, spouse, daughter, employee–which can quickly add up to be a burden too heavy to hold, depleting your happiness.

This chapter's craft project is about choosing what you carry. Creating and using a canvas bag you've decorated with meaningful quotes and images acts as your cue to notice your heavy expectations and to choose hope instead. At any time you can decide to not pick up your expectations of what should be, choosing instead to travel light, leaving you hands free to embrace more hope and happiness.

Coaching + Craft Project Supplies:

- A light-colored canvas bag, like what you can find at Joann's or Michael's Art Supply, or online at totebagfactory.com
- Fabric paint and markers
- Paint brushes
- Various rubber stamps and stamp rollers
- Shallow dishes for the fabric paint
- A piece of cardboard, approximately the same size as your canvas bag
- Ribbon
- Fabric glue

Place the cardboard inside the bag so your paint and markers don't bleed through.

Decorate the bag as you like using one or more of the art tools listed above: stamp hearts; write quotes; draw spirals with markers; glue ribbons around the edges; paint flowers, ivy, animals, or whatever inspires you.

"Motherhood has a very humanizing effect," says actor Meryl Streep. "Everything gets reduced to essentials." Whenever you use the canvas bag, think about what expectations and social comparisons you can choose to leave behind so that you place only the essentials in your bag.

For more ideas and inspiration about Choosing What You Carry bags, go to thewellcraftedmom.com/coaching-craft to see finished examples of bags created by moms in our Coaching + Craft groups.

Chapter Three

Say No to the Book Fair

"Don't let the urgent crowd out the important."
Mary Pipher

I'd said yes to too many things, made too many commitments, and overloaded my schedule to its breaking point. And now I was paying the price. I had been asked to volunteer for the school's annual book fair taking place the week after my sons' three-week school break. "The chairperson just needs a little extra organizing help," said the president of the PTA when we talked after school one day in March. "You are the perfect person," she told me. "It won't be that much of a time commitment. A breeze, actually." Flattered, I said yes.

Now, it was week three of spring break. We were out of town, spending a few relaxing days at the coast. But I wasn't relaxed. I had been put in charge of getting parent volunteers for the book fair and no one was responding to my emails. The only volunteers on my spreadsheet were me and a partially committed mom for Monday after school. I needed three or four volunteers for each of the five days of the fair, and three more for the evening hours during Math Night on Wednesday evening. The book fair chairperson was emailing me daily, asking for the schedule.

"It's just a book fair," my husband said, hovering, waiting for me to finish.

It wasn't just a book fair. I had made a commitment and I was letting people down. Letting people down appeared to be a theme: my boys had been out of school for two weeks and I had failed miserably at keeping them occupied with activities that didn't involve an electronic device. They disliked camps, the sitter was in school until 2:30 every day, and my work schedule was jam-packed with clients I was accommodating by fitting them in whenever I could, beginning as soon as the sitter arrived and working later and later into the evenings. I wasn't making the grade as an activities director, volunteer coordinator, wife, mom, or any of my other roles.

And now we were on vacation at Point Reyes National Seashore, at a cute little lodge along Tomales Bay. The sun was shining, and we had planned a scenic drive followed by a hike to the lighthouse, but I was frantically pecking away at my laptop, mad at the chairperson, the PTA president, and every single mom at the elementary school.

But I was mostly mad at myself.

"When we don't make rules and boundaries for our lives, all sorts of situations, relationships, and problems make their way into our lives," says Melody Ross of the Brave Girls Club. "And instead of living the life we really want to live, we are constantly managing all sorts of things that we really don't even want."

It's hard to set those boundaries and say no, especially to people you love or people to whom you feel obligated. People are wired for social connection; a sense of belonging is an evolutionary demand that has been passed down for millennia. When you say no, you run the risk of feeling like an outcast and being treated like one, too.

How to Be a Hybrid Mom

Women and men are wired differently when it comes to the word *no*. It turns out that women have a harder time saying *no* than men do, a difference that is present even when personality factors like agreeableness and conscientiousness are taken into consideration, according to a study of gender differences on saying *no* in the workplace that was conducted by Katharine O'Brien as a postdoctoral research associate at the Baylor School of Medicine. O'Brien's study also found that when women did say *no*, they were judged more harshly than their male counterparts, receiving lower performance evaluation scores and fewer recommendations for promotions, and they were considered less likable.

Saying *no* makes people very uncomfortable, so much so that they'll go to extremes to avoid saying it. One research study published in the journal *Personality and Social Psychology Bulletin* showed that when random strangers were asked to deface a library book by writing "pickle" in ink on one of the pages, half agreed to do so rather than saying no.

It's much easier to acquiesce and say *yes*. There are many good reasons to agree to do whatever is asked of you—the desire to be liked, respected, included, and employed, just to name a few. However, when you say *yes* to random work assignments that increase your workload but not your promotability, volunteer commitments that feel more like busywork than soul work, or favors for neighbors that feel like unwilling acts rather than goodwill, you lose time you could be spending with your family, the energy to focus on a project that feeds your passion, or the space to simply rest. Continually saying *yes* when what you really want to do is say *no* is like never taking your foot off the gas pedal, always speeding down the freeway, rushing to get from Point A to Point Z, and pulling all your obligations behind you in an overloaded trailer.

What if you could parent like a Prius? When you drive a hybrid car, the battery recharges every time you brake so you can go farther on your tank of gas. Even when you simply ease up on the gas pedal in a hybrid car, you replenish the battery. Parenting like a Prius means touching your foot on the brakes every now and again, or simply slowing down to recharge your internal battery, so you can do more with less energy.

Being a hybrid mom means saying *no*, setting boundaries on your time, and not agreeing to do what doesn't replenish you.

This can be hard to do. Especially when friends, family, and the PTA president expect you to be a regular fountain of help. "Momentary discomfort is better than long-term resentment," writes Brené Brown, author of *Daring Greatly* and *The Gifts of Imperfection*. "Daring to set boundaries is about having the courage to love ourselves, even when we risk disappointing others."

Different ways of saying no affect people differently. A study published in the *Journal of Consumer Research* showed that shifting how you phrase your no from *I can't* to *I don't want to* increases your sense of empowerment and commitment and your ability to resist temptations to sacrifice your sacred time. *I can't* creates the sense of being out of control; *I don't want to* puts your decision in the realm of personal choice.

O'Brien from the Baylor School of Medicine found that when women were given two strategies on how to handle requests for their time, either by saying, "Let me think about that and get back to you," or by regarding the request from the perspective of what advice they'd give their best friend, they had an easier time saying no. The "let me think about it" answer was the most helpful when they wanted to respond negatively but were feeling uncomfortable saying no.

"Let me think about it" is the most powerful phrase you can incorporate into your personal lexicon. This statement lifts your foot off the accelerator, and buys you time to truly evaluate whether baking three dozen cupcakes by tomorrow for your daughter's preschool feels more like barreling down the freeway or slowing down. Maybe baking is a break from the stress of your daily responsibilities. If so, say yes and start cooking. If not, realize that it's okay to say no. Really. It can help to blame external circumstances, like "My schedule is so full with this monster project at work," or to be honest about what you want and don't want to do by saying "I have time to pick up cupcakes from Safeway, but I don't have time to bake."

The year after the book fair that interrupted my vacation, I was asked to volunteer again. "We made such a good team," said the book fair chairperson. I didn't need to say "Let me think about it." I remembered that sunny morning in the sweet little lodge at Tomales Bay, shook my head, and said "No, thank you."

Saying no–and easing up on yourself–is just as necessary and important as regular maintenance is for your car. And aren't you ready for a little tune-up?

Practical Advice – Say No without Feeling Like an Outcast

We have a deal-breaker question in our family: "Does it feed your soul or feed your family?" How we answer this question is how we decide what gets added to our busy family-of-four lives and what doesn't. Work commitments, short- and long-term goals, continuing education interests, hobbies, fitness, and the like must either replenish my husband or me, or those time commitments need to nourish our family financially. Even the boys' soccer sign-ups, drum lessons, martial arts classes, and other after-school activities get evaluated by the same parameters. An endeavor with a high ticket price, whether the price is in dollars or time, needs an equally high commitment.

"Feed my soul, feed my family?" is the question I ask myself when I receive a request for a speaking engagement, when an e-course catches my attention, when I'm inspired by new ideas for programs, books, and classes. There's only so much of me, and only so little time and energy to share. The answer to that question shifts my response from ambivalent to unequivocal. "Each time you set a healthy boundary, you say 'yes' to more freedom," writes Nancy Levin, author of *Jump … and Your Life Will Appear*.

Here are some great ways you can you set boundaries, say no, and take back your time.

Practice makes peaceful. The more you say no to what you don't want, the easier it becomes. It can even help to practice saying no when you're alone, or semi-alone with your small children. Brené Brown says she bought a silver ring that she twists as she rehearses saying no. "I'll often say, to no one in particular, 'I can't take that on' or 'My plate is full,'" writes Brown in an oprah.com article. "Like many worthwhile endeavors, boundary setting is a practice."

Buy yourself some time. As Baylor School of Medicine researcher O'Brien found in her study, women who said "Let me think about that" to a request for their time felt less stress and guilt when they eventually said no.

Set limits on the time you are available to help. Setting clear boundaries on how much time you can dedicate to a project can save you from being buried in an avalanche of obligations. Explaining your time constraints in the beginning benefits both you and the people asking for your help: you benefit because you've made a commitment to yourself of how much you're willing to give, the other people benefit because you've let them know what to expect. You can set limits by saying "I'm heading to work in an hour and I'm happy to help until I have to leave," or "Filling in for you this one time works, but I don't have the time to participate on a regular basis."

Be kind to the person asking and to yourself. Adjusting your tone of voice as you say, "No, thank you," will help ease the sting of your negative response. Also make sure that you are kind to yourself, and aren't beating yourself up for declining a request for your precious time and energy.

Stand like a lady boss. A study at Harvard University found that people's dominance hormones (testosterone) were elevated and stress hormones (cortisol) lowered after standing in a power position for two minutes. The reverse was true after participants stood in a low power position. The power positions used were open stance postures (widespread limbs and increased physical space; think Superman). Low power positions were closed postures (contracted shoulders with arms folded inward). Researchers found that deliberate postures affect the brain, shifting mood, confidence, and control, and the benefits can last for several hours. Study participants who stood in power poses for two minutes prior to a mock interview were evaluated higher and deemed more likely to get the job. So when you need to say no, set boundaries, or stand out and shine, find a private place to pose like a superhero for a few minutes and watch your power grow.

Coaching + Craft – The Key to Saying No

The key to saying no is reminding yourself that your time has value and you get to decide how to spend it. If you're accustomed to being a "people-pleaser," it will be helpful to have a reminder that saying no to what you don't want means that you're saying yes to what you do.

Coaching + Craft Project Supplies

- Swivel lobster claw clasp
- Three to four skeins of embroidery floss in colors of your choice
- Four to six large hole beads
- Metallic embroidery floss (optional)
- Scissors

Find the end of one of the colors of embroidery floss and cut two pieces approximately 18 inches long, being careful not to snarl the skein of floss.

Fold one of these threads in half to create a loop. Place the folded loop through the ring at the bottom of the lobster claw. Take the ends of the piece of thread and pull them through the folded loop. Pull the thread tightly around the ring.

Add beads to the thread by stringing both ends of the embroidery thread through the holes in the beads.

Place the three or four skeins of embroidery floss horizontally on your work surface. Loop the threads at the end of the beads around the center of the embroidery floss skeins and tie a knot.

Fold the two sides of the embroidery thread skeins down. Take the second 18-inch piece of embroidery thread and wrap it five or more times around the top of the skeins, about one-quarter inch below the beads, creating a tassel. Tie the thread in a knot and trim the edges. If you're using the metallic thread, wrap the metallic thread over the tied embroidery thread at top of the tassel. Tie the ends of the metallic thread in a knot and trim the ends.

Smooth down the threads in the tassel and trim the bottom of the tassel to make the bottom even.

Like Brené Brown's silver ring that reminds her to "choose discomfort over resentment," you can use your tassel key ring to remind yourself to step on the brake, ease up on the gas, and say no so you can make time for what matters most.

This craft was inspired by Kim Purvis of madeinaday.com. You can see instructions and examples of key rings from our Coaching + Craft gatherings at thewellcraftedmom.com/coaching-craft.

Chapter Four

Take Your Time

*"We either make ourselves miserable or we make ourselves strong.
The amount of work is the same."*
Carlos Castaneda

My stomach grumbled and I looked at the clock. The fact that it was rapidly approaching 5:00 filled me with dread. It was dinnertime, and soon everybody would be hungry, not just me. I did a quick assessment of the two boys. About three minutes earlier, I had dropped the older one on the couch and turned on the television in the hopes that Dora, Boots, and Backpack would distract him from what looked like an imminent temper tantrum. The baby was in his swing, happy for the moment, but rubbing his eyes, looking sleepy. I calculated how much time it would take to breastfeed the baby, do the burp-and-wait routine, and then put him down to sleep. Could I fit it in before the older one got too hungry and unhappy? If I gave my older son a snack now, would I spoil his supper? Could I breastfeed the baby in the family room while the television was on or would he be too distracted?

I quickly arranged carrot sticks and celery sticks on a dinosaur-shaped plate and put some hummus in a little bowl with tiny T-rexes decorating the outside. I enticed my older son to the table with the promise that he could watch television while he ate (just this once I told myself, trying to quiet the Mean Manager's voice in my head). I got the baby from the swing and a pillow from the couch, sat down next to my older son, and started to breastfeed. The baby latched but quickly turned his head to check out my older son's slurping sounds as he sucked hummus from a stalk of celery. Dora and Boots sang the backpack song and my older son sang along. The baby latched and looked, latched and looked, and I leaked milk down into my nursing bra and onto my lap. At some point, I would have to change clothes for the third time today. My stomach grumbled again, and I remembered that I had eaten goldfish crackers and string cheese for lunch. I had promised myself that I'd eat more during the baby's nap time, but I got too busy catching up on laundry and trying to organize the toys into baskets while playing trains with my older son. I did a mental inventory of what was in the refrigerator and came up with nothing that looked like dinner. I couldn't remember when my husband said he'd be home, but maybe he could pick up take-out on his way. My phone was nowhere in sight, and breastfeeding made it hard to move.

"Hey, sweetie?" I said enthusiastically to my older son. "Do you want to play Find Mommy's Phone?" He gnawed on a soggy celery stick, his eyes not moving from the television screen. "If you find Mommy's phone, I'll give you a cookie." He looked up, nodded, and as he climbed off his chair, his elbow caught the edge of the dinosaur plate and bowl and they smacked the floor hard, sending vegetables and hummus flying. Startled by the loud noise, both kids started to cry. There was hummus everywhere— under the table, on the chair legs, the wall, my son, and my pants.

My husband came home while I was on my hands and knees cleaning up, the half-fed baby crying in his swing, the hummus-encrusted older son back on the couch watching Dora, the front of my shirt damp and sticky. "Why don't you tell me what's for dinner and I'll get it started," he said in a kind, even voice, the voice that trainers use to calm wild animals at the zoo. But that's the thing: I didn't know what was for dinner. How could I plan a meal when I couldn't even control five minutes of my life at a time?

What's on Mom's Plate

"I think that mothers feel more stressed because they assume the role of household managers and bear the major responsibility for childcare and housework," says Shira Offer, assistant professor of sociology and anthropology at Bar-Ilan University in Israel, quoted in an article on foxnews.com. Offer is the author of a study that links stress with the mental labor of thinking about and planning the details of household and family responsibilities. "Mothers are also the ones typically held accountable and judged for how their children fare and households are run," noted Offer. "This makes family care overall a more stressful and negative experience for mothers than for fathers."

Offer's study found that mothers and fathers spend about the same amount of time doing "mental labor," thinking about their jobs or family-related tasks and their ability to accomplish them. But there was marked differences in the effects of mental labor between the genders: mothers' mental labor had a negative effect on their well-being, which wasn't the case for dads. And moms thought more about work—in-home chores or out-of-the-house responsibilities—during their free time than dads did during theirs.

It's the multitasking moms do that messes up free-time thinking. Mothers are about twice as likely as fathers to simultaneously perform household and childcare activities. A United Kingdom study showed that two-thirds of all women surveyed admitted to multitasking at least once every hour. Nearly 50 percent admitted to doing more than one thing "pretty much all the time." Almost every mom surveyed said they were interrupted daily and 30 percent of the mothers in the study said that interruptions and reprioritizations happened all the time.

And all of this has a cost. The effects of multitasking have been compared to being high without the high. Multitasking creates confusion and distraction, decreases memory and attention, reduces productivity and the ability to think clearly. When mothers multitask at home and in public, they find doing more than one thing at one time more stressful than fathers do.

When you think you're multitasking, you're actually not. The brain "only takes in the world little bits and chunks at a time," says Earl Miller, neuroscientist at the Massachusetts Institute of Technology. Multitasking is actually more like playing a sped-up version of hopscotch–your brain can only stay in one square at a time. Jumping rapidly from one task to the next tires the brain. Each activity, large or small, drains the same amount of brain power, whether you're choosing a pediatrician for the new health insurance plan, or choosing whether to dress the doll in a pink or purple dress during playtime with your daughter. Bouncing back and forth between mental tasks, demands, and decisions activates the production of the stress hormone cortisol, which creates even more confusion.

If you're a habitual hopscotcher, once the competing demands for your attention are completed, you might find it increasingly difficult to focus on doing just one thing. It's as if you've turned on the many-tasking switch in your brain, preventing you from going back to a more peaceful and productive single-tasking state. Hooked on the many-tasking high, you may find yourself checking your Facebook newsfeed at the dinner table, mentally creating your shopping list during yoga class, or texting a girlfriend while pushing your daughter in the swing at the park.

Studies have shown that single-tasking leads to greater productivity, improved creativity, and greater output. But who has time for that when the whole family is hungry and you're on your hands and knees on the floor cleaning up hummus?

I needed a plan, a program, a recipe for making things better. But when I looked at mealtime, housekeeping, organization, decluttering, childcare, and scheduling, everything as a whole seemed too daunting and I couldn't decide where to dive in. "Starting an unpleasant task is always worse than continuing it," write authors Chip Heath and Dan Health in the book *Switch: How to Change Things When Change is Hard.* They theorize that the long-term goal may be too far away to generate short-term motivation. Starting a small, focused effort creates a better chance for a favorable outcome. "When you engineer early success, what you're really doing is engineering hope. Hope is precious to a change effort."

I needed some hope. Hope that I could keep the house clean, figure out what's for dinner ahead of time, stay on top of the mess instead of drowning in tasks that all needed to be done right now. I needed hope that I wouldn't default to the same route I had followed so often it felt like a deep rut in my mind: start a project with big ideas and high expectations but lose motivation and progress only a few days in.

"Do what you can, with what you have, where you are," said Theodore Roosevelt. I wrote the quotation on a sticky note and put it up on the refrigerator. This seemed as good enough place as any to start.

Opposing Forces

University of Virginia Psychologist Jonathan Haidt says in his book, *The Happiness Hypothesis*, that we have two different forces at work in our brains: the Elephant, which is the emotional, instinctive, interested-in-the-short-term-payoff part of you; and the Rider, the rational, realistic, future-focused part. The Elephant and the Rider often work well together, like when you launch a well-executed clean up effort because company is coming. But when the Elephant and Rider disagree, like when the Rider wants to spend Saturday morning cleaning house, and the Elephant wants to sit on the couch and rest while your husband takes the kids to the park, the Elephant almost always wins. "Changes often fail because the Rider simply can't keep the Elephant on the road long enough to reach the destination," write Heath and Health. "To change behavior, you've got to direct the Rider, motivate the Elephant, and shape the Path."

To direct the Rider, realize that you're not disorganized, just overwhelmed without a clear path of knowing where to start. Pick one room and start there. When my house was full of toys scattered every which way, the kitchen counter was piled with half-finished projects, and the surface of my desk couldn't be found under the clutter, I picked one part of the family room and went to work on cleaning, organizing, and moving the toys and baskets back to the boys' room. I created a small sanctuary in the family room where my house felt like my home again, as long as I didn't engage my peripheral vision. I could sit in the corner of the couch, look out over the deck, open the windows, listen to the sound of the fountain and the birds in the backyard, and find a moment of peace.

To motivate the Elephant, understand that you're not lazy, you're exhausted trying to keep your Elephant on task. Your Elephant isn't interested in your long-term goal of having a place for everything and everything in its place, so she will fight every large-scale plan to get there. But if you give your big Elephant small, achievable things to do—like clearing one corner of the room—she gets to throw her weight around and things get done, slowly but surely, one step after another.

To shape the path to get you where you want to go, recognize that you're not a mess, you just need helpful habits that will help you stay on track. If your goal is to make mealtime easier, gradually introducing a system of recipes, shopping lists, and meal plans will make the process much more simple to implement. If your goal is to have the toys organized, committing time every day to sort through the mess and fill a box of outgrown toys to donate will get you closer to a job well done. Even better, if your kids are big enough, create a clean up checklist for them to follow—pictures work just as well as words—that lists the steps involved in cleaning up: stuffed animals back on the bed, Legos in the bucket, cars and trucks in the big bin.

"Moment by moment we choose and sculpt how our ever-changing minds will work," writes Michael Merzenich, a pioneer in brain plasticity research and the author of *Soft-Wired: How the New Science of Brain Plasticity Can Change Your Life.* "We choose who we will be in the next moment in a very real sense."

Practical Advice – Take Small Steps

When you leap onto a new goal that's big and exciting, it's like jumping onto your emotional Elephant. It feels good to be taking big steps, going in what feels like the right direction, feeling like you're large and in charge. But your Elephant gets easily bored, becomes discouraged when progress is slow, stops in her tracks when the going gets tough. And instead of making progress toward your big goal, you end up back at square one, kicking yourself with those big elephant feet for failing yet again.

Long-term success comes as the result of many small steps, not a few giant ones. Your emotional Elephant doesn't have the patience to wait around for the fulfillment of a long-term goal, like a completely clean house or a down-to-the-details two-week dinner plan with a dozen recipes destined to be family favorites. Your impatient pachyderm needs immediate rewards that come from small successes: dividing an elephant-sized goal into tiny turtle-sized steps.

"We can all break up any goal into many teensy-weensy turtle steps," writes author and columnist Martha Beck in her blog at marthabeck. com. "No matter what you're facing today, whether it's churning through a ridiculous 'to-do' list or trying to fix Africa, take one little step up. Tomorrow, take another one. Inch by inch, you'll lift yourself all the way up."

Right now, think about a project that feels overwhelming–the great piles of brightly colored plastic toys in the kids' bedroom or the stacks of paperwork on your desk that you keep avoiding because you don't know where to start. Instead of resigning yourself to the thought that there's too much to do so you don't do anything at all, pick just one project, one pile, one piece of the mess that you dread doing and set the timer for five minutes. For five minutes all you'll do is dig into the mess, whether it's putting toys away or filing paperwork. Housekeeping guru Marla Cilley, a.k.a. The FlyLady, calls this "The 5-Minute Room Rescue." You get as much done as you can in short five-minute bursts of energy and attention, preventing your petulant pachyderm from procrastinating.

Your room rescues are just like how most people save for college for their children–in small installments made to 529 accounts over time, not in one giant-sized deposit. In the same way, you can start saving your sanity with small incremental steps toward your organized desk, easy-to-follow meal plan, or tidy playroom. When the timer dings, you're done. As the Spanish saying goes: "Poco a poco se va lejos" which means "Little by little, one goes a long way." Schedule a few five-minute Room Rescues a day to satisfy your rational Rider, and to keep your emotional Elephant happy, motivated, and rewarded. Because when your elephant feels rushed or overloaded, all 6,000 pounds of her stops in her tracks.

Coaching + Craft – Celebrating Small Steps with Fancy Flip-Flops

"Going fast, we can only do what we already know. There is no room for the new," writes Anat Baniel, creator of the NeuroMovement Method and author of *Move Into Life*. "Slow is how we discover what it is to feel and be vital and alive, to fully participate in the dance of life."

To celebrate the slow steps you'll take toward your larger goals, this chapter's Coaching + Craft project is creating fancy flip-flops, pretty reminders to enjoy the unhurried, easy way toward your goals.

Coaching + Craft Project Supplies

- One pair of inexpensive flip-flops
- One yard of ribbon
- Fun and fancy decorating embellishments like fabric flowers, sparkly jewels, rhinestones or even buttons
- Glue gun and glue sticks (I recommend the type of glue sticks made for flexible projects.)

Starting at the back of one side of the Y-shaped strap, glue the end of the ribbon on the underside of the strap. Wrap the ribbon around the strap in overlapping layers, finishing at the toe. Cut the ribbon and glue the end to the top side of the strap so the glue doesn't irritate your foot. Repeat the wrapping process on the other side of the strap.

Glue your embellishments on the top of the flip-flop strap in any way that pleases you—one single flower at the toe, many small sparkly gems sprinkling the strap, playful dots of buttons all in a row.

Every time you wear your fancy flip flops, remember to map the steps for your Rider and keep the pace slow for your Elephant. As French poet Charles Baudelaire wrote: "Nothing can be done except little by little."

This chapter's Coaching + Craft project was inspired by Martha Stewart. For more ideas and inspiration, go to thewellcraftedmom.com/

coaching-craft to see finished examples of fancy flip flops created by moms in the Coaching + Craft groups.

Part 2
CRAFT

Carve Out Time For Yourself
Remember Why You Fell in Love
All About Guilt
Find Friends
Talk Nicely

*"When you see someone putting on his Big Boots,
you can be pretty sure that an Adventure is going to
happen."*

A.A. Milne

Chapter Five

Carve Out Time for Yourself

*"If we take care of the moments,
the years will take care of themselves."*
Maria Edgeworth

It was close to 2:00 a.m. I had finished the feed-burp-wait routine, and the baby was finally asleep next to me in bed. I had put him midway between my husband and me but the baby had inched closer and closer to the warmth of my body. I had absentmindedly given him more and more room so I was now perched along the very edge of the bed, fully engrossed in my book, reading by the dim glow of a nightlight.

I had spent the whole day shouldering the burden of being a mom to my toddler–enticing, bribing, reprimanding, yelling, cajoling, prodding, rushing, wheedling, planning, telling him to eat his peas, stop touching his brother, let me tie his shoes, hold still, open his mouth so I could brush his teeth. Alongside that, I felt physically drained by the limitless demands of the baby, from breastfeeding on demand to his determined attachment to attachment-parenting and to being held all the time. But now it was my turn, and my time to give myself a well-earned reward. I knew I'd pay dearly tomorrow for delaying sleep tonight, but I rationalized away the loss of sleep: it was just one hour added to many nights of too little or too-interrupted sleep. I was exhausted already when I woke each morning, I told myself. I deserved to lose myself in a book, to read until my eyes were so heavy I couldn't keep them open. It was finally my chance to do what I had been wanting to do all day, but couldn't because my kids came first.

But finding me-time at 2:00 a.m. felt like giving myself the same amount of space I had on the bed–little and leftover, crowded out by what I gave to my children.

Everything Changes

A mother's desire to care for her child is like an addiction. Studies have shown that the sight and smell of your baby lights up the feel-good center of your brain like alcohol, drugs, or chocolate. Research using MRI brain imaging shows that a mother's brain reacts to her baby in an eerily similar way to how an addict's brain reacts to getting cocaine. Both the baby and the drug create a dopamine release that encourages the mom and the addict to repeat the same behavior that triggered dopamine in the first place. Nuzzling your child's head, playing peek-a-boo with the baby, and cuddling your child up close are all ways that your baby gets you high.

Becoming a mother literally changes your brain: after giving birth, gray matter becomes more concentrated in the hypothalamus, parietal lobe, prefrontal cortex, and amygdala, making you more attuned to your baby's needs. Hormones like oxytocin, estrogen, and prolactin find eager receptors in your expanded brain, generating a positive feedback loop that continues the cycle of rewards, motivation, and positive emotions, bonding you to your baby in powerful ways.

But there are downsides to this intense attachment to your child. Parenting drains your resources: the physical depletion from sleep deprivation and breastfeeding; the emotional wear and tear from worrying about childcare, financial strains, medical issues, or marital stressors; and the uncertainty about your choices and how they affect your child's development. You are determined to be a good mom. But your definition of what a good mom looks like may be constricted by perfectionism and high expectations, preventing you from giving yourself permission to enjoy activities that would fulfill you outside of work and family.

One study showed that a full 80 percent of mothers surveyed didn't spend any time on self-care, even though nearly 100 percent of mothers said they felt better when they did. Employed mothers today spend more time doing primary childcare (where the child is the main focus of attention) than non-employed mothers did in 1975. Sociologists Suzanne Bianchi, John Robinson, and Melissa Milkie, who wrote *Changing Rhythms of American Family Life*, examined time-use diaries from 1965 to 2000 to uncover how people spent their time. The authors discovered that to make room for the additional hours for childcare, mothers have cut back on the amount of time spent doing housework, curtailed time spent with spouses and friends, and all but erased their free time.

I believed I had to *earn* my enjoyment, and so I put off pleasure until all the laundry was done, my children were asleep, and the toys were put away. But feeding everyone else's needs before taking care of my own was like eating a diet of only scraps. And I was starving.

It was my fault. My all-or-nothing mentality about self-care meant that it needed to be significant to matter–like a massage, an hour-long dance class, or several hours alone strung one after the other like Christmas lights. If my free time was just a small moment, just one twinkly light of 20 minutes or less, I thought it wasn't enough to brighten that long, dark corridor of parenting where I frequently got stuck. Instead of reading, writing, or dedicating some time for myself, I would fill those smaller chunks of time with chores. Without regular activities that replenished me, I became more and more tired, depleted, and resentful.

Something needed to change. My husband helped when he could, but he was busy building his business. My mother came when she could, but she was too far away to provide daily assistance. I found a card with a quote from Mother Theresa that said "Not all of us can do great things. But we can do small things with great love." That quote joined the Roosevelt sticky note on the refrigerator. I started a practice of doing small things for myself every day and found that when I did small things with great love for myself, it was easier to do the bigger things for my family. The small things came with these big lessons:

Take your time. Time for self-care as a mom will often come in smaller pieces than it did before children–think night lights, not flood lamps. You can schedule time for the significant, brilliant events that replenish you, like a girls night out, date night, or weekend getaway, but to keep yourself from being depleted, you'll need little bright spots to light you up every day. Knowing and doing what lights you up–even in the tiniest of ways–can continually replenish your energy and emotional resources.

Make a *Time Well Spent* list. When there's a spare five, ten, or 30 minutes, mothers often default to doing chores. There are always tasks to keep you busy. But even a well-spent minute can restore your energy, nurture your soul, create inspiration for what to do when you have a bigger piece of time available. Developing your Time Well Spent list can be challenging because of how self-sacrifice is imbedded in the Good Mom definition. "Many women are so wrapped up in what we should want that we don't know what we do want," writes Regena Thomashauer in her book *Mama Gena's School of Womanly Arts*. "We don't know how to call forth our dreams and don't know how to recognize or voice them."

Making your Time Well Spent list is how you discover what you want so you can find the time to create it. Begin with making a list of three things that would replenish you if you had one minute, five minutes, ten minutes, or 30-minute windows of time to fill. An artistic client has bookmarked websites that she browses for ideas and inspiration. Another client checks her list of journal prompts in an app on her smart phone and writes for a few minutes. One client has committed to drawing or sketching for 30 minutes every day, mostly in many small bursts, not big stretches of time. You could listen to inspirational books during your 30-minute commute, bookmark short instructional videos highlighting various dance techniques on your smart phone and practice in the kitchen, or call a close girlfriend who lives far away. Even a moment spent daydreaming about where you'd go on a getaway can replenish you.

What will light you up is very individual. Only you know where to plug in the night light when you're feeling tired and lost in your own dark corridor of parenting.

Here are a few more ideas to help get you started on your Time Well Spent list.

One minute: For one minute, practice a breathing technique called Heart Rate Variability, as suggested by psychologist Rick Hanson. Developed by the HeartMath Institute, this breathing exercise has three steps: breathe so that your inhalations and exhalations are the same length; imagine that you are breathing in and out from your heart; and then bring to mind a memory or experience of love, gratitude, or awe. Research shows that breathing in this way harmonizes the intervals between heart beats and initiates the relaxation response, which not only benefits both your cardiovascular and immune systems but increases your happiness overall.

Five minutes: Once you get into the multitasking mode, it can be hard to slow down. Movement meditation can calm your brain and your body. Move to music, do a series of yoga poses, or practice Tai Chi. When you relax your body, your mind tends to follow.

Ten minutes: Create a crafting box you can play with when you have a little bit of time and then easily pack up once the baby wakes up and your creative time ends. Use partitioned plastic lunch containers and fill them with art supplies. Some ideas include a Bead Box with a variety of beads, stretchy cord, and small scissors, and a Sketch Box with colored pencils, small unlined notepads, and erasers.

Thirty minutes: Nap. Really. Many times when you're feeling overwhelmed, it's because you're not getting enough sleep. There's a reason why life coach and author Martha Beck tells her team to "Go lie down!" at the first sign of any stress. Sleep restores. Sleep rejuvenates. Sleep gives you the superhuman strength to take on any challenge, from colicky infants to the crankiest of toddlers.

All self-care isn't created equal. There's a qualitative difference between what you choose to fill your time with and how it affects you afterwards. When you're creating your Time Well Spent list, it's important to find activities and people that nurture and inspire you and bring out your very best self so that you emerge happier, with a full pantry of energy to share.

Activities that allow you to check out mentally, like television, internet shopping, or light reading, can shut down your thinking but they don't normally nurture your mind. Afterwards, you might feel cheated or uninspired, like you've wasted precious time. However, sometimes investing time in a mindless activity is a necessary blessing, like when you're overwhelmed and exhausted. When you need to unwind because you're overstressed, mindfully choose to check out, and acknowledge that the activity will create an empty bubble where you can relax, but that you probably won't feel replenished afterwards. Once you're more rested, see if you can schedule time to do an activity from your Time Well Spent list, so you can fill up your energetic and emotional resources.

Self-care is a mirror. How well you replenish your inner resources depends greatly on the strength of your support from family and friends; the depth of your resources of babysitters, preschools, and playdates; and your willingness to let other people help you. Leaning on your community allows you to fill up your pantry with what sustains you, which in turn gives you more energy and enthusiasm to share with your family and friends.

"Giving yourself some loving attention is not selfish. It is sensible," writes author and Reiki Master Penelope Quest. "If you feel loved and cherished, even if it is only by yourself, then you will have more love to give to others, too."

You have to make self-care happen. It's not anyone else's job to know what you need. You have to make self-care your own priority: carve out time for it, figure out what you're going to do when you have it, and insist on taking it.

During couples counseling years ago, I realized that I felt depleted nearly all the time. As an introvert with two active boys, I needed time when no one needed me. Finding alone time was challenging: my husband worked from home; there wasn't space in the house for me to set up a quiet corner for creative work; even the bathroom wasn't private because once I shut the door, everyone from the toddler to the cat wanted in. With the counselor's help, my husband and I negotiated one morning a week when he would leave the house, take our older son to school, and take our younger son to his program at the Rec Center. Then my husband would work from a coffee shop, giving me three lovely hours alone.

It was bliss and continues to be–my alone time remains on my husband's and my shared calendar. And even though my extroverted husband didn't understand in the beginning why I needed the house all to myself, he willingly complied because he could see the benefits: happy wife, happy life.

Self-care requires some sacrifice. It can be hard to relax when there's a long list of what needs to be done. Taking time for yourself takes practice–and perhaps clearing out a corner in your home where you can ignore the rest of the mess temporarily. You might have to choose: clean house or me time? Or simply prioritize. Knowing you'll have more energy and focus after spending time caring for your inner self rather than for everyone else, start with what you really want to do, whether it's jewelry, art, or a nap, and then do chores afterwards, fitting in whatever tasks you can in the time that remains.

It takes effort to remember what sustained you before kids and then figure out how to fit those bright spots into that dark, narrow corridor of being a mom. It's a challenge to find what nourishes this new you within the parameters of parenthood. It can be even harder to ask for the time you want, and then harder still to take it. But it's necessary and important. "Taking good care of your family is no different than taking good care of yourself," writes Karen Maezen Miller in *Momma Zen*. "There is nothing more gratifying. There is nothing more immediate. There is nothing more available. Every day is a good day to take care. Every moment. This moment."

Practical Advice – Stop, Drop, and Roll

You may think you don't have any time for yourself. And that's probably true. You don't have any time away from small children who need you, from work that wants more time from you than you have to give, from a spouse who's waiting for you to finally look up and notice him or her again. But following a three-step process called Stop, Drop, and Roll might help you to create more time for yourself within your busy schedule.

Stop doing what isn't essential. Write down everything you do, handle, manage, plan, or coordinate. Then be ruthless as you take a close look at your list of chores and your outside responsibilities and eliminate what isn't necessary, saving to the list only what must be done. What is on your list because it's part of your definition of being a good mom? What would it be like to let it go in exchange for more time for yourself? This process is like releasing ballast from the basket of a hot air balloon. If you and your family are quickly losing altitude and on the verge of crashing, what can you throw overboard so you stay aloft?

Drop what can be done by someone else. You don't need to be the one who does it all. You can pay for a housekeeper to come every other week or trade your special skills for a home-cooked meal. Hire a "task rabbit" to assemble your son's new toddler bed. Grocery shop online and have it delivered. Use Amazon Prime's free delivery for almost everything on your shopping list. Sign up for delivery of prepared meals or organic produce. Then ask your spouse for help, and see if there's a way to divvy up the remaining chores and put self-care on the schedule for both of you.

Roll with it. How can you put wheels on what isn't working well so that you glide along a bit more gracefully? Even if an unwanted task remains on your have-to list, it doesn't have to be so bad. Listen to music while cleaning up. Drink chai tea while carpooling. Talk with your girlfriend on the phone while folding laundry. Combining something that isn't so pleasant with something that delights you doesn't make more time for you but it will create more enjoyable time overall. And that can light up a room.

Coaching + Craft –
Lighting Your Way with Votive Candle Holders

A pretty candleholder can be your reminder that self-care moments often come as little bright spots in what seems like an endless hallway of tasks and responsibilities. This candleholder is simple to make, and can be decorated with any combination of colors.

Coaching + Craft Project Supplies

- One or more small glass cups or jars large enough to fit a votive candle. Look at thrift stores or craft stores to find shapes and sizes you like.
- Tissue paper in various colors, cut, torn, or paper-punched into small pieces
- Matte Mod Podge glue or basic school glue
- Paint brush
- Scissors
- A paper punch (optional)
- Votive candles

Cut the tissue paper with scissors, tear it, or use a paper punch to create circles or other shapes (depending on your paper punch).

Put your Mod Podge or glue in a small dish and water it down just a little so the glue will adhere to the glass cup but won't drip. Using the paint brush, apply glue to one area of your glass votive holder and stick tissue paper to the glass, applying another coat of glue to the top of the paper. Continue to glue tissue paper to the outside of the votive holder in an overlapping pattern, making sure to brush another coat of glue to the top of the tissue paper as you go. Once the glass cup is covered, allow it to dry before placing a votive candle inside.

Even though your bright spots of self-care moments might be as small as a flickering candle, you can still make these little moments count.

To see pictures of votive candleholders created by moms in Coaching + Craft groups, visit thewellcraftedmom.com/coaching-craft.

Chapter Six

Remember Why You Fell in Love

"A successful marriage requires falling in love many times, always with the same person."
Mignon McLaughlin

Every now and again it happens–my sleep falls apart and I'm wide awake at 3:00 a.m. for no particular reason. When my boys were younger, there were always reasons: fussy babies, breastfeeding, nightmares, the occasional tumble out of bed. Sleep deprivation was a constant companion for my husband and me. But on this night the house was quiet. Everyone was sleeping soundly. Everyone except me.

I was on day six of little sleep. I felt like my brain was wrapped in heavy wool. I could only hold onto tiny scraps of patience for my boys and none whatsoever for my spouse. And my usually soft-spoken manner was replaced by the demeanor of a potty-mouthed, irritable shrew. I felt like I had lost several layers of socialization, and this, as you might expect, wreaked a wee bit of havoc on my marriage.

In the kitchen, while packing up school lunches for the boys, I commented to my husband that every rough patch in our relationship corresponded to a time when I wasn't sleeping well. When he asked me what exactly I meant by that, I didn't have an answer other than a random fact pulled up from a dim corner of my brain, which I said out loud: "Correlation does not imply causation." When he looked at me weirdly, I shrugged. I was in an insomnia-induced brain fog; nothing made sense.

But there was some truth to the causation comment. In the past, I was so willing to take the blame for the problems that arose in my marriage (well, maybe not on the outside in the midst of an argument, but definitely on the inside where self-blame and shame made themselves at home). Owning the responsibility for all of the problems in my relationship was like wearing an itchy, too-tight sweater all day long. I wove this "I Suck" sweater from my beliefs about what a good mom should do and what a good wife does. A good mom puts her children first, stays calm, plans activities, and doesn't forget sunscreen. A good wife attends to her husband, sets his needs before her own, asks about his day, and actually listens to his answer.

My sweater grew tight when I snapped at my husband after his "home in five" turned into 40; when we slipped into a familiar spat about finances because I couldn't contribute to the household account as much as I had promised; when I said, "I'm just too tired tonight" to his bid for affection, again. My itchy sweater was my daily reminder of all the ways that I fell short.

Couples counseling sessions helped to halt the downward tumult of our marriage when it got really rocky. One big shift came when our intuitive therapist made it abundantly clear that one person cannot be responsible for all of the problems in a marriage. Neither my husband nor I believed her at first. We were both pretty sure that the problems in our marriage originated with me. If I could only be happier, more mellow, more relaxed, less judgmental, more easygoing, and less anxious, everything would be just swell. But the counselor insisted that the problems in a marriage are always the product of the people in it, like fabric woven with two different kinds of fiber. The push and the pull of our relationship was the two of us trying to blend, adjusting to tension from within and outside our relationship, and working on untangling the knots together.

Are All Parents Unhappy?

It's a common belief that children initiate an unavoidable downward slide in marital happiness. The research is mixed on whether or not this is actually true. "Whether or not children go hand in hand with happiness depends on many factors, including our age, marital status, income and social support, as well as whether our children live with us and have difficult temperaments," writes Sonja Lyubomirsky in a *Psychology Today* article. Lyubomirsky and a team of social psychologists conducted a research study to look closely at the relationship between parenting and wellbeing. They found parents of young children, and parents who are under 25 years old, tend to be less happy than other married parents, empty nesters, and dads in general. But they also found that each relationship is so different, with its own stressors, tensions, and reoccurring and unresolvable spats, that it's impossible to compare one marriage to another.

A research study by The Enduring Love Project places the blame for marital unhappiness squarely on the shoulders of married couples, not their children. The study, funded by the Economic and Social Research Council, revealed that married parents didn't invest the same time and effort into maintaining their relationships as did childless married participants. Married men and women with children were less likely than childless couples to spend time together, engage in shared activities, say "I love you," and have open conversations with one another. Married parents were more negative than childless couples about the quality of their marital relationship. And in a very telling result from the research, fathers listed their partners as the most important person in their lives; mothers listed their children.

You might be putting off scheduling a date until your baby sleeps through the night, until after you find a trustworthy sitter, or until you get through this busy phase at work. Happily ever after might feel so far away that you don't know where to begin the journey to get there.

Relationship psychologist and author John Gottman recommends specific activities you can do to build trust, connection, and commitment in your marriage, which add up to around five hours each week. Five hours is a lot of time when you're already overwhelmed, but any small effort will generate significant results. "If you're in a relationship now, you can use that relationship as a laboratory to experiment with new behaviors," writes Dr. Harriet Lerner, author of *Marriage Rules: A Manual for the Married and the Coupled Up*. "It takes two to tango. It takes only one to make things a whole lot better."

You begin with one of the following 5C's: connect, create clear expectations, carve out couple time, coax in the Kind Caretaker, and concentrate on the little things. Just start with one, and discover what new findings develop in your relationship as a result of your experimentation.

Connect. In relationships, partners make small efforts to connect throughout the day, engaging in what Gottman calls "bids." These requests for attention can come in many different forms, like your husband talking about a frustrating coworker, commenting on the ball game, or sharing a story about your son. And in the moment he makes his bid you have a choice: do you nod your head and say, "Uh huh," and continue with what you were already doing, or do you stop what you're doing, make eye contact, and really listen? When you're tired, distracted by the children's needs, and overwhelmed by your long list of chores, your husband's bids can be annoying, pulling you away from your other priorities. But repeatedly giving small gifts of your time and attention to your spouse fills the well of your relationship you both can draw from when times get tough. "Trust is built in very small moments in which one person turns toward their partner when they are in need," writes Gottman.

Create clear expectations. Disagreements are created and resentment builds when expectations aren't clear and the workload feels unbalanced. The only way out of feeling disappointed, resentful, or upset is to work it out. Schedule a meeting with your spouse, make a long list of the chores, ask for help, get clear on what you both want and how to work together to make it happen. According to the authors of *The National Marriage Project's report, 2011 State of Our Unions: When Baby Makes Three: How Parenthood Makes Life Meaningful and How Marriage Makes Parenthood Bearable*, there are significant benefits for doing so: "Women are more likely to report that they are sexually satisfied when they report that they share housework with their husbands. What happens outside of the bedroom seems to matter a great deal in predicting how happy husbands and wives are with what happens in the bedroom."

Carve out couple time. Couples who go out on a date at least once a week are three times more likely to say they are very happy together, as compared to couples who don't spend time together as a couple. The National Marriage Project's study found that couples' commitments to spending time together without their children led to stronger marital stability and increased overall satisfaction in the marriage. And when couples with a new baby kept up their pre-baby commitment to couple time, they were much less likely to experience a decline in the quality of their marriage. Do you think date night is too expensive? See this chapter's Practical Advice section for ideas on how to make it more affordable.

Coax in your Kind Caretaker. It can help to have an outsider's perspective on the problems in your marriage. A session with a wise counselor can provide a place for expressing frustration and annoyance to a compassionate listener and obtaining new ideas on how to come to terms with what isn't working. Counseling can help you and your spouse to find ways to more frequently fill up the well of good feelings in your marriage, get out of the rut which takes you from the start of a disagreement to a full-blown fight, and be mindful of how the words and tone you use affect your happiness. Like Leo Tolstoy said: "What counts in making a happy marriage is not so much how compatible you are, but how you deal with incompatibility."

If finding outside counseling isn't in the cards for you for one reason or another, you can allow your inner Kind Caretaker to improve your marriage. A study published in *Psychological Science* discovered that recruiting the perspective of the Kind Caretaker, what researchers called a neutral third party, had positive results. In the study, 120 couples were observed over the course of two years. In the first year, all couples experienced a decline in marital happiness. In the second year, half of the couples were taught a 21-minute intervention technique–a journal-writing activity that couples did three times over the course of the study's second year. Every four months, the couples wrote about a recent upset in the marriage from the perspective of a neutral third person who wanted only the best for everyone involved. Journal prompts asked the questions: "How might this person think about the disagreement? How might he or she find the good that could come from it?" The couples were asked to try to practice this outsider's perspective in their daily lives, especially when in the midst of a disagreement with their spouses.

Couples in the control group, who weren't taught the intervention technique, continued their steady decline in marital happiness over the course of the second year. The well-being of couples who practiced the journal writing activity stayed stable and they experienced the added benefit of feeling less stressed after disagreements with their spouses, even though they fought just as much as the couples in the control group.

Concentrate on the Little Things. Small acts of kindness, like foot rubs, taking the heavy basket of laundry upstairs, and leaving sweet messages on sticky notes, can generate a big impact on your marriage and create what researcher W. Bradford Wilcox from the University of Virginia calls *generosity*. His study found that the happiest couples are the most generous couples: 50 percent of people who ranked high in generosity reported their marriages as being very happy; only 14 percent of people who scored lower on generosity evaluations claimed to have very happy marriages.

To create and maintain a happy marriage, Gottman recommends a minimum of a five to one ratio of positive to negative: at least five positive acts of kindness, generous words, and loving moments with your partner for each negative comment, criticism, or disconnected interaction. Think small acts of kindness rather than expansive gestures: truly listen and offer sympathetic responses to your husband's story of his hard day at work, stick a little love note to the bathroom mirror, or buy his favorite cookies at the grocery store.

"Marriages aren't healed with big things; they're healed with small things done every day," writes Dr. Kelly Flanagan, clinical psychologist and author of the book *Loveable: Embracing What Is Truest About You, So You Can Truly Embrace Your Life*. "They aren't healed by doing new things. They're healed by doing old things we used to do and quit doing somewhere along the way. And, if we can set aside our ego for a little while, we don't need anyone to tell us what those things are. We already know."

Practical Advice – Making Date Night Affordable

My oldest son was 18 months old when my husband and I went out on our first date night. We had been talking about it for a long time, but always ended the conversation without a date night scheduled because we didn't have a sitter. One day at the playground at a local park, I watched a young woman cheerfully managing two toddlers, dealing with sandy fingers in the boy's mouth, the girl's whining about wanting to go home, and tussles over ownership of the blue shovel. Transfixed, I watched as she patiently tied shoes, retrieved the scattered sand toys, and loaded the two kids in the wagon and headed off. It was only after she was out of sight that my sleep deprived brain shouted "Sitter!" and I kicked myself for not asking for her phone number.

The next day, I saw the little boy from the park at my son's first day of nursery school. His mom generously shared the sitter's phone number and I called that night, scheduling her for the following weekend. On our date, my husband and I reminisced over dinner, held hands on the way to the movie theater, and remembered why we liked each other. But we ended up spending more than $100 for one night of reconnecting, which wasn't a workable plan for going forward. We needed a way to continue date nights without the hefty price tag. Here are some of our ideas:

Cheap date. Look into your local museums to see if they have evenings when the museum is open late with free admission. Search for art gallery openings for a way to enjoy a free, culturally inspiring night out. Enjoy dinner at a friend's (and return the favor at a later time). Schedule your sitter during the day and go for a hike, relax on the beach, or pack a picnic and go to the park. If you belong to a gym, you could put your child in the gym's daycare (sometimes for a minimal fee), and work out together or swim in the gym's pool.

Babysitting Swaps. Explore ways to get free childcare, like swapping with friends or asking parents or other family members to help. Many mothers' groups have babysitting co-ops, where you earn points by watching other parents' children and redeem them when those parents watch yours. Or you could earn childcare hours in exchange for one of your special skills, like cooking, organization, or party planning. When I worked as a massage therapist, I traded massage sessions for childcare. An acupuncturist friend does the same.

Discount dates. Online deals can help you to save money on date night activities, like dining out, cooking classes, couples massage, wine tasting, and more. Be aware of expiration dates and limitations before you purchase deals, so you can be sure you'll be able to use the promotion before it expires.

Break time. Getting creative with your time can be a way to turn break time into date time, like meeting for lunch during a regular work day when the kids are in school or daycare. My husband and I have flexible schedules, so we meet every Friday morning for a coffee date after dropping the kids off at school. We talk about upcoming vacation ideas, plan our next date night, sync our schedules, and simply talk to each other to find our way out of the co-parents/roommates rut.

In-home special. Staying home but making it special can turn any night into a date night. My husband I used this trick often when the children were very young and our budget was very small. You and your spouse can cook dinner together, watch movies, and treat yourselves to popcorn and candy, or drink wine on the deck under the stars. Candlelight brings romance to any meal, even leftovers. The point is to create time together to reconnect and that can be done anywhere, even at home. Make plans, put them on the calendar, and commit to reconnecting, rekindling, and remembering why you fell in love in the first place.

Coaching + Craft – No Impossibilities
Dream Catcher

"In dreams and in love there are no impossibilities," wrote poet Janos Arany. This Coaching + Craft project can be a talisman to remind you to dream, plan, and protect your marriage with small, intentional steps.

Traditionally, a dream catcher is placed above the head of the bed, ideally where morning light will shine on it. Native American folklore claims bad dreams get caught in the web and then dissolve in the light of day; good dreams slide down the feather to enhance the nighttime journey of the dreamer. This is how your relationship can be: a beautiful circle you've woven that dissolves the bad, creates room for the positive, and gives you the marriage of your dreams.

Coaching + Craft Project Supplies

- One embroidery hoop ring, any size
- Lace or open-weave fabric
- Ribbon or yarn in various colors
- Beads with holes big enough to thread the ribbon through
- Feathers
- Items that have meaning for you in your relationship

Open the embroidery hoop and put the lace or open-weave fabric in between the two circles and close the hoop. Trim the fabric on the outside of the embroidery hoop so that the edges are neat. Weave the ribbon in and out of the fabric in a pattern that pleases you–there's no right or wrong method. String beads onto the ribbon as you weave it through. You can tie pieces of paper to the dream catcher with sayings that have special meaning in your marriage or mementos from happy times in your marriage. When you are pleased with the result, knot the ribbon to the edge of the embroidery hoop, snipping off the loose end.

To hang the feathers from the bottom of the dream catcher, tie a piece of ribbon to the feathers and then string beads on the ribbon, pushing the beads onto the shafts of the feathers. Repeat with more feathers and two or three additional pieces of ribbon. Tie the end of the ribbon with the feathers and beads to the bottom edge of the hoop and repeat with additional beaded feather strings.

Dream catchers, because they're made up of many twists of the ribbon through the fabric, can be your reminder that even the most knotted of things can be beautiful.

This dream catcher project was inspired by Decoist and Hayseed Homemakin'. Come see examples of dream catchers at thewellcraftedmom.com/coaching-craft and get ideas and inspiration for your own.

Chapter Seven

All About Guilt

"There's no problem so awful that you can't add some guilt to it and make it even worse."
Bill Watterson

My kids' summer was so short. Because of our older boy's year-round schedule at his elementary school, the summer break from start to finish was only four weeks long. Before summer break started, I made a list on the white board in our kitchen with ideas for events, activities, family trips, and other excursions we could do together during our four precious weeks. I made spreadsheets for each week, detailing when I could work, see clients, and write. I blocked off Wednesdays and Thursdays on my calendar so the boys and I could spend those days on outings, and I adjusted my schedule so I worked with clients only in the evenings on those days. I scheduled the sitter to come earlier on her two afternoons each week.

I had a plan.

Over the short summer break, we visited science museums and the zoo and camped twice in the mountains with friends. One night, we pitched a tent in the backyard and made s'mores by roasting marshmallows over charcoal briquets in the barbecue, and then slept in the tent until the sprinklers woke us up. We swam in my brother-in-law's pool and watched a handful of movies. We rode the train to a nearby town for a special lunch and played in a park before climbing aboard the train for the ride home.

It should have been a great summer, despite its brevity. But for me it wasn't; I spent the summer trying to follow an unmanageable plan. Without enough time built in to manage my business, I couldn't keep a clean division between work and family. In the midst of what should have been fun time with my family, I checked email when the boys were engaged with exhibits at the science museum, scheduled clients as the boys brushed sheep and fed goats at the children's zoo, and scribbled notes for the blog in dark movie theaters. I answered emails from my laptop during lunchtimes, and returned phone calls on the way home from outings once the little one had fallen asleep in his car seat. I worked frantically while the sitter watched the boys, trying to cram a week of work into a few hours. I was relieved to discover that both campsites had wifi.

When the first day back to school arrived, and I was packing my son's lunch and helping him load up his backpack, I felt guilty. Our summer had been average, nothing spectacular compared to other families' European vacations or Hawaiian adventures. I felt guilty about my work, too. Projects, calls, and emails had piled up over the last four weeks because I had worked so little.

But my biggest guilt came from remembering my divided summer. All throughout the summer break, I wiggled whatever work I could into every crack of time I could find. When I was with my children, I was only halfway present and wholly distracted.

Sociologists call this mental pollution "contaminated time." Contaminated time is when you're doing one thing (like spending "quality time" with your kids) but simultaneously thinking of all of tasks that are still undone. It's unpleasant, toxic thinking that increases stress and reduces happiness because it's impossible to fully enjoy what you're doing when you're trying to be two places at once.

My contaminated time sullied my whole summer.

Mommy Guilt

Guilt is the language of parenthood most moms speak very well. In The Working Mother Research Institute's report *What Moms Choose*, more than half of employed moms and 44 percent of stay-at-home moms reported feeling guilty about the household mess. Nearly 50 percent of working moms and 42 percent of stay-at-home moms felt guilty about not taking care of themselves. And more than half of employed moms said they felt guilty that they weren't spending enough time with their children. A full 94 percent of moms in a BabyCenter survey admitted to experiencing guilt about something, from how little time they spent with their children to using television as a babysitter.

In a study conducted by the website workingmomsbreak.com, the top answer to the question "What's the hardest part of being a working parent?" was, not surprisingly, "Guilt that I can't do everything well."

An informal survey by Amy Ransom, author of *Surviving Life and Motherhood (Just)*, found that moms felt most guilty about not playing with their children enough, letting kids watch too much television, not spending enough quality time with their children, losing their tempers with their children, and always saying "In a minute" to buy time to work on other things, rather than attend to the child's request.

Guilt grows out of perfectionism, out of an imbalance between the desire to do everything well and the reality that you can't. It's inspired by a misguided expectation of how much you need to achieve in order to feel a sense of accomplishment at the end of the day, despite the workload you bring home and the overload your home creates.

Perfectionism and guilt jumpstart a cycle that's a lot like a roundabout with no way out. Perfectionism to do more drives guilt that you're not doing enough. Guilt leads to exhaustion when you try to accomplish more and overwhelm when you can't. Exhaustion and overwhelm join forces to generate disappointment and more guilt about not doing enough. This is a cycle that can make you feel lost and empty, still going around and around the guilt-exhaustion/overwhelm-disappointment-more guilt roundabout with a carload of unmet expectations by the end of the day.

But if you can look at the discomfort around the guilt and really see where it's taking you, guilt can motivate positive growth. Guilt can drive you to a happier place. It can be your Cadillac for change. "In the end, what we really need in life is not more *comfort*, but an unshakeable belief in our ability to handle *dis*comfort," writes psychologist Kelly M. Flanagan.

Using your guilty discomfort to create change comes from asking three questions: Is your guilt realistic? Can you let it go? What can you do to make it better?

Is your guilt realistic? It's easy to get stuck by comparing yourself to other moms or to a high standard that is impossible to meet. Performing a reality check on your expectations can ease your guilt. Is it true that you need to have a clean-enough-for-company house all the time? Is it true that putting your child in the daycare at the gym while you ease your aching body into the jacuzzi means you're a bad mom?

A Google search can help with your reality check by reinforcing the knowledge that other moms share your concerns or by leading you to information that assuages your guilt. For example, a study published in *The Journal of Marriage and Family* found that the amount of time parents spent with their children between the ages of three and 11 had no influence on children's academic achievement, behavior, and emotional well-being. A Harvard study found that adult daughters of working mothers had completed more years of formal education on average and the adult sons of working mothers spent more time on childcare and household chores. If you're feeling guilty about working outside the home and not spending more time with your children as a result, these statistics might ease your discomfort.

Can you let your guilt go? Guilt often arises out of the "not enough" mentality—not having enough energy to continue to try to breastfeed when it isn't going well, not using cloth diapers instead of disposables, not cooking a homemade meal but going through the drive-thru instead. The only way out of the "not enough" quagmire is to acknowledge the enough-ness of what you are doing and the value you bring to your family. "When we can let go of what other people think and own our story, we gain access to our worthiness—the feeling that we are enough just as we are and that we are worthy of love and belonging," writes Brené Brown in *Daring Greatly*.

What can you do to make it better? Guilt can be a strong motivator for building and maintaining strong relationships with the people close to you. "Feeling guilty is a way of showing that one cares," writes Roy Baumeister in a study on guilt published in *Psychological Bulletin*. Your guilt may be a clue that you're off track, or your actions are out of alignment with your values. "We feel guilty when we hold up something we've done or failed to do against our values and find they don't match up," writes Brené Brown.

Use healthy guilt to inspire change. If you feel guilty about taking the easy, environmentally unfriendly way out, make a commitment to making one small shift, like packing a reusable water bottle in the diaper bag instead of a plastic, throw-away one. If you feel guilty about contaminating your time with your kids by bringing your working mind into your family time, make a resolution to put the smart phone away and bring your undivided attention to playtime with your children.

"The guilt we feel as mothers comes from loving our children to the moon and back. From our desire to do right by them, to be the best mothers that we can be and to give them as much of us as they deserve," writes Ransom. "So, next time you feel that pang of guilt, instead of berating yourself stop for a moment and acknowledge it for what it really is. Love. Complete and utter unconditional love. We're doing the best we can. And it is good enough."

Practical Advice – Shushing the Yeller in You

Years ago, my kids owned a book called *Superhero ABC*. Each letter was dedicated to an amusingly illustrated good guy/gal who had special powers to beat the bad guys: "A is for Astro-Man who is always alert for an alien attack… B is for Bubble-Man who blows big bubbles at bullies." The book was one of the boys' favorites, so I read it often when they were little. Each time, I winced when we arrived at the Yellow Yeller, a skinny, harried, bed-headed female superhero with her mouth opened wide in a scream, overwhelming a cowering, not-so-evil-looking bad guy. I would quickly flip through the letter Y to get to Z, afraid that if I paused too long on Y, one of my boys would point to the Yellow Yeller and say, "Mommy!"

I never felt like I was exercising superhero strength when I got to the end of my patience and yelled at my children. I felt more like V for the Vile Villain who vilifies her victims. I would manage to get through a whole day without yelling and then lose control when one son would fall to the floor for the fourth full-blown temper tantrum of the day, or when fat messy buckets of water would splash out of the tub when my wriggly boys refused to sit still, or when I felt depleted from the never-ending cycle of food-dishes-diapers.

Developing the self-control to stop yelling meant building my brain power to become the P for Patient Parent who praises her progeny. This strength came from a surprising array of sources, including sleep, food, exercise, and mindfulness, all of which affect the prefrontal cortex of the brain.

The prefrontal cortex is your brain's Controller. It makes executive decisions about what's good or bad, predicts the future consequences from your current actions, builds your expectations, and controls your urges to act out. The prefrontal cortex is fueled by glucose, which converts molecules into energy for your brain and body. Lack of sleep exhausts the supply of glucose for the Controller, depleting its executive functioning abilities and putting the Controller at the mercy of your moods. And when you're hungry or existing on a diet of goldfish crackers and string cheese, your Controller becomes like Ebenezer Scrooge–very stingy with how it doles out energy. Willpower is a costly task that drains the brain's energy supply of glucose, so the budget-minded Controller immediately cuts the resources for self-control. This leaves you more impulsive and more focused on short-term rewards, like yelling to release your frustration from the child-created chaos, rather than on long-term goals, like getting everyone to behave without losing your temper.

While getting good sleep and eating good food both improve your brain's use of glucose, physical activity helps even more, promoting the Controller to CFO. Exercise makes your brain bigger and faster, especially in the prefrontal cortex, the Controller's area of expertise. Studies of people who exercise regularly have found that they are generally less impulsive in their spending habits, more healthy in their dietary choices, more in control of their emotions, and less likely to be attached to bad habits like procrastinating, smoking, drinking–and yelling at their children.

Something else that increases blood flow to that all-important prefrontal cortex is mindfulness. Inviting mindfulness into your life isn't always about finding the time to sit still every day–although the benefits of even five minutes of meditation are huge. When you bring mindfulness into your day-to-day routine, you focus on the present moment, allowing the worry to dissolve, stepping away from the incessant narrative in your mind, and becoming aware of what's right in front of you–the sensation of soapy water as you wash dishes (again), the sparkle in your husband's eyes right before he says something funny, the shift in your daughter's cry when she sees you coming to pick her up.

Becoming the mom that you want to be–the M is for Mindful Mommy who merrily manages the mess–means taking many little steps toward a big goal. It would be lovely if you could eliminate yelling all at once, like a superhero who eradicates evil forces with superhuman strength. But growing more patience starts slowly, often with a good breakfast, and then continues from there. "A habit cannot be tossed out the window," said Mark Twain. "It must be coaxed down the stairs one step at a time."

Coaching + Craft – The Enough Box

When you spend time at the end of the day ruminating about everything that didn't get done, or when your thoughts linger in disappointments from the day, you're investing in what sociologists call overthinking. "Overthinking ushers in a host of adverse consequences," writes Sonja Lyubomirsky in her book *The How of Happiness: A Scientific Approach to Getting the Life You Want.* "It sustains or worsens sadness, fosters negatively biased thinking, impairs a person's ability to solve problems, saps motivation, and interferes with concentration and initiative."

This chapter's Coaching + Craft activity is about creating a way to counter your overthinking about not doing enough. You'll decorate a box with Washi, a semi-transparent masking tape that is available in many colors, designs, and widths. The beauty of Washi is that it's removable, making it easy to reposition the tape if you make a mistake.

Coaching + Craft Project Supplies

- Small box of any size, preferably with a lid
- Washi tape, available at craft stores or online
- Slips of paper small enough to fit in your box and large enough to include a few sentences

Decorate your box with Washi tape in any way that delights you. Once you're finished embellishing the box with Washi, cut small slips of paper and keep them in a pile near your box. Whenever you find yourself overthinking about what did or didn't get done, write a note that lists a recent accomplishment and put it in your Enough Box. Celebrate the small but mighty moments that made up your day, from the numbers of diapers changed to the number of times you took a big breath and then managed to hold your temper, from making dinner to making eye contact with your child while he shared the details of his day.

Your notes in your Enough Box can help you feel **good enough** when you're feeling like you're **not enough**. Pull out your accomplishment notes when you find yourself feeling guilty or stuck in a compare-and-despair mood. Keeping track of your accomplishments can keep what didn't happen that day from overpowering the beauty of what did: you, showing up to save the day.

Visit thewellcraftedmom.com/coaching-craft to see examples of Enough Boxes made by moms in Coaching + Craft groups.

Chapter Eight

Find Friends

"Call it a clan, call it a network, call it a tribe, call it a family. Whatever you call it, whoever you are, you need one."
Jane Howard

I didn't want to take the boys to the Friday morning playgroup at the church down the street, but knew I should. The playgroup was just a few minutes away. The more my children interacted with others, the better they became at taking turns, being nice, and following the rules. Well, in theory. The two previous times we had attended the playgroup, it didn't go well. We hadn't been asked to leave or to never ever return–it was a church group, after all–but my spirited boys didn't win any awards for good conduct, no matter how hard I tried to instruct, direct, and encourage them to behave.

The day was sunny and warm. I thought that if my older son walked and released some energy before heading into the church auditorium where the playgroup was held each week, he'd have more self-control. We were running late today, though, so the younger one would need to ride in the stroller. I pulled the stroller from the garage to the entryway and went looking for my younger son. He was hiding behind the half-opened door to the pantry and took off running when he saw me. I picked him up and used my mommy voice over his *no no no no no no's* to remind him of the cars and trucks, games and puzzles, singing and story time at the playgroup as I carried him toward the stroller. His no's grew louder and turned into shrieks as I put him in the stroller and strapped him in the five-point harness. It was like putting a straightjacket on a monkey. A very mad monkey.

We made our noisy way down the street to the church, my son's angry wails radiating from the stroller. We passed by other moms in the church parking lot as they unfastened their compliant, quiet children from their car seats. I felt pangs of envy for them, which I'm sure were not reciprocated. This was not getting off to a good start.

When we entered the church courtyard, my younger boy remembered the cars and trucks and changed his screaming to cries of *out, out, out, out*. As my older son ran off into the auditorium, I quickly unbuckled the little one and set him free from his stroller. The playgroup was a child's paradise, with toy stations throughout the room and a big round rug in the center where story time would happen a little later.

Even though I wasn't religious, I prayed that today wouldn't be a repeat of the last two times we had come, when I'd hear a kid cry and it would be because my older son had taken away a toy from another child, or hit someone, or was hogging all the cars and trucks.

As I feared, some kid cried and I flinched, quickly looking around the room to find the problem. A small boy clutched one end of a toy firetruck as it was being yanked out of his hands by a bigger boy—who wasn't mine! I breathed a sigh of relief as I watched a tired-looking mom hurry to the tussle to mediate. Everyone else stared, too, and I could see other moms shaking their heads in disapproval.

The red-faced mom forcefully pried her son's fingers off the firetruck and handed it back to the other boy, who smiled triumphantly before walking away, the firetruck held close to his chest like a well-earned award.

I sat down next to the mom on the floor in the midst of the plastic cars, trucks, and tractors. "I bet it will be my son who makes the next kid cry," I said by way of introduction. The mom smiled gratefully, we exchanged names, and pointed out our children. She had two boys, the same sizes as mine. We immediately bonded over our bad-mom status, sharing horror stories of our boys hitting, grabbing, even occasionally biting. We confessed our love-hate relationship with the playgroup: how we loved that it was a fun, free place to bring the boys, but hated the embarrassment that came with feeling like the mom who couldn't control her children. We heard a child cry and we both laughed, certain it was probably one of our boys causing the commotion. But it didn't feel as bad anymore. I still felt like I was in the penalty box for my son's bad behavior, but I had a teammate sitting next to me. I wasn't alone.

The Lonely Ones

About 60 percent of moms report feeling lonely and loneliness is particularly highest when moms are parenting children under five years old. Part of a mom's loneliness is related to confinement—moms are tied to the house by their children's nap times and feeding schedules. Getting out of the house can be a production as well: loading up the diaper bag with sippy cups, snacks, bottles, diapers, wipes, the favorite toys, pacifiers, extra changes of clothes, and other supplies; making sure the children are dressed, dry, and wearing shoes; checking to see that you're basically clothed, wearing a bra, and not stained or sticky.

Before having children, many women think it will be easy to make friends after the baby comes, like a baby is the entry code into a secret club where all mommies bond over shared stories of diaper blow-outs, temper tantrums at Target, and unreasonable expectations from the mother-in-law. But that sense of sisterhood between moms can seem far from the lonely reality that you might be experiencing, especially if you believe that your challenges aren't shared by other parents and think all the other moms passed Motherhood 101 with flying colors compared to your failing grade. A mom's keenly developed need to make sure she isn't perceived as a failure can keep her from sharing how hard parenting really is and make it difficult to find true friends.

In addition, there is often a strong similarity between high school cliques and mommy groups—many moms already have their inner circle friends, and aren't interested in letting anyone new into the club.

This could be because each of us has our own red velvet rope, keeping the number of friendships at a fixed number. Robin Dunbar, an anthropologist and psychologist who studies primates, determined that the size of primates' social groups directly relates to the size of their brains. For humans, that number is about 150 people. This is what's referred to as the Dunbar Number, a maximum number of people with whom you can maintain stable, interpersonal, face-to-face friendships. Dunbar created smaller cliques within the 150 club: 50 close friends, 15 inner circle confidantes, five intimate companions.

So if you're getting the brush-off from another mom, it might be because her Dunbar Number has reached its maximum allowance. She doesn't have room. Still, it's important to have someone by your side, someone to help you to feel like the journey isn't so arduous—literally.

Students at the University of Virginia, outfitted with a weighted backpack and standing all alone at the base of a hill, estimated that the incline was steeper than it actually was. Once they had a friend beside them, the hill didn't seem so steep. The longer that friends had known each other, the less steep the hill appeared. The same perception is true of parenting: when you're struggling with the daily challenges of motherhood the mountain of the day can look pretty steep. A friend can make the journey seem shorter, much easier, less of an ordeal you need to endure all by yourself.

A good friend can help you to be a healthier person, and a better person all around. If your friend eats healthfully, chances are you will, too. If your best friend exercises regularly, you're more likely to, as well. Having friends improves sleep, increases immune system functioning, and lowers blood pressure and cholesterol. A best friend at work leads to a seven-fold increase in how engaged you are with your job.

Friendships make you happy. "The very best thing that can happen to people is to spend time with other people they like," writes Daniel Kahneman in an article on Gallup, Inc.'s website. Feelings of well-being increase when you spend time with friends, whether you're an introvert or extrovert. Close friendships are so important that married people have rated close friendship with their spouse as five times more important than physical intimacy.

It's an interesting phenomenon that when couples get married, they often tend to isolate themselves from friends, which can create loneliness, even within the marriage. Loneliness is on the rise, with a three-fold increase over the last 20 years of people saying they have no close friends. A study in 2004 reported that most Americans typically feel close to two people, a decrease from 1985 statistics when people claimed three. Low numbers of friendships (less than four seems to be when people slide into the danger zone) can have dire consequences, and has been compared to "smoking 15 cigarettes a day or being an alcoholic, more harmful than not exercising, twice as harmful as obesity." Why people fail–or feel like failures–is because they feel unloved and unaccepted.

You may not feel outcast or unloved–you have your spouse after all–but he may not understand why you're missing a close confidante so keenly, and may not be able to fill that void for you. Women's and men's friendships are typically different: women interact face-to-face, keenly observe one another's body language, and make eye contact; men's friendships tend to be side-by-side–think sports-watching. It can be hard for your spouse to give you what a good girlfriend knows how to do naturally.

There may be physiological reasons for these gender differences. A study by the University of California, Los Angeles, suggests that when women experience stress, they release the hormone oxytocin, which triggers a tend-and-befriend response, not the fight-or-flight reaction that stress elicits in men. And when a stressed woman engages with her friends and tends to her children, even more oxytocin is released, which produces a calming effect, a hormonal response that doesn't occur in men.

Friendships are needed to create a place of caring for yourself and others. Friends are necessary, especially during the stressful years after kids come into the picture. "What saved me is that I found gentle, loyal and hilarious companions, which is at the heart of all meaning: maybe we don't find a lot of answers to life's tougher questions, but if we find a few true friends, that's even better," writes Anne Lamott in *Stitches: A Handbook on Meaning, Hope and Repair*. "They help you see who you truly are, which is not always the loveliest possible version of yourself, but then comes the greatest miracle of them all–they still love you."

Practical Advice – How to Make Friends

Sometimes you'll get lucky. You'll meet another mom in your childbirth preparation class, hit it off (spouses included), and remain friends forever. Or your neighbor has a baby within a few months of yours, and you find yourself at her house more often than your own. But it may take more effort to build your inner circle. It can be a lot like dating, only this time you're looking for another mom to share your experience. Making the effort to make new friends can be scary, because you have to be vulnerable to reach out to another person. You run the risk of being rejected. It's challenging, because you might need to flex your social muscles to extend your social circle. And hard, too, to find the space to make friends in the middle of what already feels like a full house of sleepless nights and busy schedules.

But close friends are a beautiful mirror, reflecting back to you who you truly are. So, if you're far short of reaching your Dunbar Number and have fewer than four friends you can call close companions, remind yourself that reaching out to build your social support circle benefits your mental and emotional health.

Here's a little how-to advice:

Do stuff. To meet potential friends you need to step away from social media and leave your house. Online friends rarely turn into face-to-face ones; social media sites tend to be better frameworks for maintaining the friendships you already have. Research supports what you probably already know—that real life connections are necessary to build the trust that is essential for a solid friendship.

You can meet other moms through your child's activities: join a playgroup offered through your local mothers' club, attend mothers' club meetings and activities, enroll your child in a co-op preschool, or go to the park. Or indulge a hobby by taking an in-person class, joining a MeetUp activity, or establishing your own group. When the boys were younger, I created a group called BOYS-terous for moms of only boys. I coordinated regular playgroups at the park, which created wonderful ways for the moms to connect while the boys played.

Be brave. When you meet a mom who you think would make a good friend, take a deep breath, flex your courage muscle, and start a conversation. Or you can bravely inform your friends that you're looking to add more mommies to your friendship base. It can take a particular kind of courage to reach out to make new friends. As Rachel Bertsche observed in her book *MFW Seeking BFF: My Yearlong Search for a New Best Friend*, it's culturally acceptable to announce that you're looking for a mate but far less so to admit that you need friends, "Letting on that you could use a new BFF implies loneliness, and if you say you're lonely you might as well say you're a shut-in."

It also takes courage to invite a potential friend into your imperfect life and run the risk of rejection. "We're afraid that our truth isn't enough—that what we have to offer isn't enough without the bells and whistles, without editing, and impressing," writes Brené Brown in *Daring Greatly*. But if you don't show up as you truly are, any mom you meet will only be a fill-in and not a true friend.

Play house. You don't need to bring the new friend all the way into your life all at once. Just as you wouldn't invite a brand new friend into your most private room in the house, you wouldn't invite her to hear your most private thoughts at your first meeting either. Manage your intimacy with friends by thinking about what access they would have to various parts of your home: a family room friend would be a close ally, a master bedroom friend would be your nearest and dearest. You wouldn't want to confide your marital troubles with a mom who's just a front yard friend. And you certainly wouldn't share your feelings of failure with someone who was a stay-on-the-sidewalk acquaintance. Deepening your friendships is a process that develops slowly. Share your thoughts, desires, and dreams with friends based on mutual trust. And you can kick them out the door and deadbolt it behind them if they disrespect or disparage you.

Diversify. Social scientists call it *multiplexity* when you create an overlap of how and where you engage in a relationship. You create overlapping links when you invite a mom from the neighborhood playgroup (a uniplex relationship) to your monthly book club meetings. Or when you host a home-cooked meal for a few preschool parents and their families. Building multiplexity, which extends a friendship into wider aspects of your life, deepens the relationship. It's like inviting an acquaintance, someone who has been only a front porch friend, into your kitchen for a cup of tea.

Repeat. Making new friends can be a lot like dating: you have to meet a lot of people in order to find a few who you really like. But keep up the work of being brave, playing house, and extending your friendships into other parts of your life and soon you'll find other moms to welcome onto your porch, into your family room, and to sit at your table and enjoy your company.

Coaching + Craft- Be the Magnet

"There is a magnet in your heart that will attract true friends," wrote spiritual leader Paramahansa Yogananda. When you trust that you have something valuable to offer in a relationship, you can attract friends like metal to a magnet. This chapter's project is a fun way to integrate this knowledge with a hands-on project.

Coaching + Craft Project Supplies

- 3/4-inch flat, clear gems from your local crafts store or 3/4-inch acrylic cabochons (from a resource like Tap Plastics)
- 3/4-inch round magnets
- Magazines
- Scissors or 3/4-inch round paper punch
- Silicon glue

Cover your work table with newspaper to protect the surface.

Go through old magazines to find pictures, colors, and words that represent what you bring to your friendships and the qualities you appreciate in a friend. Use the magnet to trace a circle around the images and use the paper punch or scissors to cut them out.

Glue the magazine pictures onto the magnets with the silicon glue. The glue can be messy so you may want to use a flat toothpick to apply a small amount to the magnet. Let the glue dry for five minutes.

Apply more glue to the center of the picture on the magnet, and press the flat gem to the top. Let the glue dry completely before sticking the magnets onto your refrigerator.

These magnets make great gifts. You can package them in little metal tins you can purchase online. Make a handful to give to your brand new friends.

To view photographs of magnets made by moms in Coaching + Craft gatherings, go to thewellcraftedmom.com/coaching-craft.

Note: The gems and magnets in this project can be a choking hazard for small children. Please keep these craft items—and others listed throughout the book—out of reach of children who are still in the stage of putting bright and shiny objects into their mouths.

Chapter Nine

Talk Nicely

"Be mindful of your self-talk.
It's a conversation with the universe."
David James Lees

When my younger son was three and a half, he went through a rough patch and I did, too. Right alongside his noisy, messy tantrums, I had private ones of my own. Whenever he fell to the floor in a heap, I heaped up my thoughts of what I must be doing wrong.

I could often see my son's tantrums growing, like a mean, little dragon hatching inside of him, bursting forth with frustrated energy that overtook his body, emotions, and self-control. When his dragon raged, I would take him to one of the bedrooms and sit on the floor with my back against the door. I'd wait while he struggled with his anger and tried to pull me away from the door with all of his mighty three-year-old power. I hated this battle that repeated itself daily. I resented the time and energy it stole from me and my time from my older son. I'd spent hours researching and creating a long list of ideas of what to do, but hadn't yet found a workable solution.

Meanwhile, my inner Mean Manager made a list of her own, telling me all the different ways I was failing: *No other mom struggles like this. You're not trying hard enough. If you weren't so angry, he wouldn't be either.*

I felt like I needed help, like I had missed a few essential classes of Motherhood 101, and could use a tutor to show me what I was doing wrong, so I scheduled a meeting with a counselor at a local parent resource center. I met with the counselor in her small office at the back of the center and checked off my questions in my notebook as she answered them one by one. She gave me a worksheet on how to set better limits with my three-year-old, offered suggestions on how to thwart the tantrums, and shared ideas about encouraging him to nap (he was on a nap mutiny at the time). Her resources were variations of what I had already tried, but I felt hope trickle in just from talking to a trained professional.

I hesitated when I got to the last question on my list. "Anything else?" the counselor asked. "Um, well, what do I do if I'm not liking motherhood all that much?" I said in a nervous rush. The counselor looked confused. Perhaps I spoke too fast and she didn't understand me. I took a breath and started to repeat my question more slowly when she interrupted. "I'm not sure what you mean," she said. I stammered that motherhood was really challenging: I wasn't really enjoying it; the tantrums–sometimes up to four a day–were wiping me out; and the rewards seemed so puny for the amount of heartache and hard work involved. As I talked, I saw her face close up into a hard stony look but

I continued to explain, thinking she must have heard this before from other moms, because I couldn't be the only one feeling this way, she works in a parenting resource center for God's sake.

"So, you're saying that you don't like being a mom?" she asked, her voice dripping with disapproval.

My face grew hot as I realized I *was* the only one who didn't always like being a mom. I was all alone on this island of messed up motherhood, so far from the land of normal that no boat could ever reach me.

I stammered my way out of the counselor's office, barraged by self-talk tsunamis that would continue to batter the coast of my self-esteem for months, a full-on shame storm: *You are such a loser. What were you thinking? You've got a perfectly good life and you're too selfish to appreciate it. Buck up and put your big girl boots on. Better keep your mouth closed from here on out. Whiny baby.*

Shame Storm

"Shame is that warm feeling that washes over us, making us feel small, flawed, and never good enough," writes Brené Brown in her book, *The Gifts of Imperfection*. My shame didn't feel warm. It felt cold and polluted as it wiped out the ecosystem of my already delicate self-esteem, leaving behind an ugly flood of mean thoughts about myself. My husband could sense something was wrong, and I reluctantly shared what had happened in the meeting with the counselor. I asked him directly if he thought I was the only mom who felt like such a failure. He consoled me, saying all the right things, but I secretly feared that the counselor's disapproval confirmed what my husband had been thinking all along and what I knew deep down—that there was something really wrong with me.

I wasn't nice to myself for many months after that meeting with the counselor. Every day, my inner Mean Manager's voice was loud in my head. I didn't begin to feel better until I shared my experience with my mom friend from the church playgroup and allowed her outrage at the counselor's response to my question to warm the waters of my cold, harsh self-criticism.

Looking back, I see that my Bad Mom Island was deeply populated by pretty much everyone I knew, but some moms had permanent residences there and others only visited from time to time. "For so many of us, feelings of deficiency are right around the corner," writes author and psychologist Tara Brach in *Radical Authenticity: Embracing Your Life with the Heart of a Buddha*. "It doesn't take much—just hearing of someone else's accomplishments, being criticized, getting into an argument, making a mistake at work—to make us feel that we are not okay."

And those feelings of not okay-ness, whether you live on the island or only visit, get in the way of your happiness, your parenting, and your life.

Defense against the Dark Thoughts

Some people believe that if they tell themselves they're okay enough times, it will finally sink in. But telling yourself you're okay, when at the core you believe you're really not, is like putting a happy-face bandage on your deep feelings of inadequacy in the hopes that you will stop hurting.

Research by Joanne Wood, professor at the University of Waterloo, found that positive affirmations only work for people who already possess high self-esteem. "If a person with low self-esteem says something that's positive about themselves, but is well beyond what they'll actually believe, their immediate reaction is to dismiss the claim and draw even further into their own self-loathing convictions," writes Wood in *Psychological Science*. Her research found that positive affirmations like "I'm a good mom" can trigger reflexive, contradictory thoughts like "But I'm really not," or release a flood of examples of how that statement isn't true. Writes Wood: "Statements that contradict a person's self-image, no matter how rallying in intention, are likely to boomerang."

You have to deal with the deeper issues first.

Negative self-talk is woven into the primitive part of the human mind, what's called the reptilian brain. According to Rick Hanson, neuropsychologist and author of *Hardwiring Happiness*, our brains and our bodies are still wired to take in the negative more quickly and more fully than the positive. We experience intense pain throughout our bodies but, for the most part, we feel intense pleasure in only a few specific physical areas. Our brains produce more neural activities from negative stimuli than positive.

The amygdala, the deep part of the brain that processes emotions, especially fear and aggression, uses about two-thirds of its energy looking for the bad–both outside of ourselves and within. When found, these negative experiences go straight into storage, unlike positive events, which have to be nurtured and invited into long-term memory.

"The brain is like Velcro for negative experiences but Teflon for positive ones," says Hanson.

All is not lost to the dark forces within you, however. You have the power to change your brain to be better at noticing and appreciating the goodness that exists in your life. Here's how to use your own magic to tame your dark thoughts:

The Kind Caretaker. "Self-criticism comes from a desire to keep ourselves safe. So we first have to have compassion for the critical voice," says self-compassion researcher Kristin Neff in a *Psychology Today* article. "The self-critical voice needs to be heard, and then paradoxically it can quiet down."

Listening to the critical voice, the Mean Manager inside your head, can be challenging because of the flood of negativity that it generates. But when you call for help from your inner Kind Caretaker, compassionate listening becomes much easier. When you listen with openness, it's easier to notice how your self-criticism stems from the Mean Manager's desire to protect you from being hurt, vulnerable, and ashamed. "You're going to fail miserably," can be interpreted to mean "I'm scared that you're going to be embarrassed." Acknowledging that the Mean Manager's messages are there to protect you and keep you safe can ease the sting of your self-talk. "Caring kindly for the reptile, rather than either believing it or struggling against it, is the way out of dread and into peace," writes Martha Beck in *Steering by Starlight: The Science and Magic of Finding your Destiny*.

The Strong Guardian. A study published in *Cognitive Therapy and Research* found that enlisting the help of a third inner entity, what can be called the Strong Guardian, can disarm the Mean Manager even more. In this study, researchers divided their participants into three groups: a control group that received no intervention; a group trained to use their Kind Caretaker to self-soothe when attacked by the inner Mean Manager; and a group that enlisted the help of their Strong Guardian, an attack-resisting protector.

The participants in the self-soothing group were asked to imagine the Kind Caretaker and even visualize how he or she looked, and then write five statements from this kind perspective to soothe the distress caused by negative self-talk. The Strong Guardian group followed those same instructions for their imagined inner protector, but also wrote retaliatory statements against their Mean Manager, like "I've been letting you attack me for some time now, I'm not going to let you continue to put me down the way that you do," and "From now on, I'm going to stand up for myself when you say negative things to me."

The study found that while participants in both the Kind Caretaker and Strong Guardian groups experienced a lessening of shame, the group trained in how to use their Strong Guardian to deal with the Mean Manager significantly lowered the severity of depressive symptoms.

Naming. Naming is used in a technique from Acceptance and Commitment Therapy (ACT), which is a type of psychological intervention. This mindfulness technique, called Naming Your Stories, is about organizing thoughts by themes to ease discomfort. If much of your negative self-talk is concentrated on how you're failing as a mom, you could name that theme "Bad Mom." If your inner dialogue reminds you over and over how you are not living up to your spouse's expectations, "Disappointing Wife" could be another. With this strategy, whenever your Mean Manager starts telling a story that falls into one of your categories, you mentally drop the thought into that slot by saying something like, "There's another Bad Mom thought." This simple process moves your thinking from the primitive reptilian brain to a more highly developed part of your brain, giving you the ability to discern what's true from what's inner bullying.

Patchwork Joy. Many people believe that being unkind to themselves is the way to stay on task or get rid of a bad habit like yelling, procrastinating, or overeating. "I found in my research that the biggest reason people aren't more self-compassionate is that they are afraid they'll become self-indulgent. They believe self-criticism is what keeps them in line," says Neff, quoted in an article in the *New York Times*. The opposite is actually true. Self-forgiveness and self-compassion–especially after you've failed–increases accountability and your chances of achieving your goals.

Researchers Janet Polivy and C. Peter Herman coined the term "what-the-hell effect" to describe the downward spiral that can happen after a setback, like when you eat one cookie when you're on a diet and then say, "What the hell," and eat the whole box. "Crucially, it's not the first giving-in that guarantees the bigger relapse," writes Kelly McGonigal, describing the study in her book, *The Willpower Instinct: How Self-Control Works, Why it Matters, and What You Can Do to Get More of It.* "It's the feelings of shame, guilt, loss of control, and loss of hope that follow the first relapse ... This leads to even bigger willpower failures and more misery as you then berate yourself (again) for giving in (again)."

Self-compassion researcher Neff developed a test to evaluate self-compassion and found that people who tested high on self-kindness and understanding were happier, better adapted, and possessed a strong sense of well-being. Scoring high on self-compassion also correlated with less negativity after setbacks and less brooding following negative evaluations.

Writes Christopher K. Germer, author of *The Mindful Path to Self-Compassion: Freeing Yourself from Destructive Thoughts and Emotions*: "A moment of self-compassion can change your entire day. A string of such moments can change the course of your life."

It is possible to change your life, one compassionate thought at a time. For me, it meant learning how to gather up the Good Mom moments and string them together one by one. Self-compassion came when I acknowledged my patience and love as I sat with my upset and unhappy son while he had a tantrum, both of us managing our emotions the best that we could; when I recognized the patchwork of joy that came in unexpected pieces; and when I loved my worn, messy self.

"Thread your needle, make a knot, Find one place on the other piece of torn cloth where you can make one stitch that will hold," writes Anne Lamott in *Stitches: A Handbook on Meaning, Hope, and Repair*. "And do it again. And again. And again."

Practical Advice – Helping Others to Help Yourself

Turning your thoughts toward self-compassion can feel like the old adage of trying to sew a silk purse out of a sow's ear, especially if your Mean Manager is a big bully. But you can begin to grow happiness and kindness for yourself by first showing kindness to others. Studies have shown that helping other people can increase your connection to your community, intensify appreciation for your good fortune, provide a distraction from your difficulties, and improve how you perceive yourself, which can lead to greater confidence and optimism. Helping others can be a small as including random acts of kindness in your regular routine or as big as volunteering regularly in your neighborhood. Here are suggestions to keep you on the right path:

Not too big, not too small. It's important to get the balance just right. If helping others means that you extend yourself too far and wide, you may feel resentful or overwhelmed. Or if your acts of kindness are sprinkled here and there throughout the week, your mind may not be able to see the difference between the extra kindness and what you do on an ordinary day. Research conducted by Sonja Lyubomirsky, author of *The How of Happiness: A Scientific Approach to Getting the Life You Want*, found that happiness increases significantly if you designate one day every week as the day you do great things.

Spread your breadcrumbs wide. The human brain quickly habituates to new pursuits so if your acts of kindness are the same from week to week, the familiar path won't lead to more happiness. Adding variety to what you do—like cooking a meal for a new mom in your mothers' club one week and committing to an hour of clean-up at the preschool the next—will ensure that your kind efforts continue to fill your happiness bucket. "If an activity is meant to enhance well-being, it needs to remain fresh and meaningful," writes Lyubomirsky.

Create a community. Research has shown that if you combine your kindness with interacting with others, happiness lingers longer because your brain habituates more slowly when you are engaged with other people. "Major commitments that involve regular contact with other people ... may not lend themselves to the same degree of adaptation and may continue delivering benefits to you (and others!) in terms of happiness, self-esteem, and other resources and skills," says Lyubomirsky.

Being nice to others can be your path to happily ever after and can turn you into the happy hero of your very own life. It's like magic that builds and builds. "A single act of kindness throws out roots in all directions, and the roots spring up and make new trees," wrote Amelia Earhart. "The greatest work that kindness does to others is that it makes them kind themselves."

Coaching + Craft – Kindness Rocks

My family and I were at my favorite place in the whole world, the Fitzgerald Marine Reserve, just north of Half Moon Bay in Northern California. We had hiked the trail that hugs the bluff above the tide pools where families stepped gently on the algae-covered rocks as they looked for crabs, starfish, and brightly colored sea anemone. The trail led my husband, boys, and me along a ridge above the Pacific Ocean and through a tunnel of trees to the concrete steps that headed down to Seal Beach, a small cove linked to the reserve's tide pools.

I took off my sandals, sank my feet into the sand, and breathed in the salty air. The boys dashed ahead to the edge of the water with my husband close behind. I lingered, slowly walking while looking for that perfect stone. The rocks at Seal Beach are dark and smooth, but each one is a different size and shape. It's against the rules to take shells, rocks, and other wild things from the reserve, so whenever I'm there, I pick up a stone, carry it around for a while, rub my fingers on its smooth surface before setting the rock back down again.

Just as each stone at the shore is different from the others, so you are from anyone else. This chapter's project, Kindness Rocks, is about recognizing your own uniqueness. Kindness Rocks are made from stones that you embellish with words from your Kind Caretaker or Strong Guardian so they can act as talismans against your inner bully.

Coaching + Craft Project Supplies

- Smooth stones of different sizes, collected by you or purchased at the crafts supply store.
- DecoArt glass paint markers or Sharpie pens
- Patio Paint, colored and clear
- Paintbrushes

Wash the stones with soap and water and let them dry. Use the colorful Patio Paint to decorate the rocks with images that remind you of your Kind Caretaker and Strong Guard and then allow the rocks to dry. Then, write inspirational words or quotes on the rocks with colored markers. When the rocks are completely dry, paint them with a coat of clear Patio Paint.

Your Kindness Rocks can be lasting reminders of the benefits of listening to your wise, kind, and confident inner voices, which hopefully will sound a bit like Christopher Robin talking to Winnie the Pooh: "You're braver than you believe, and stronger than you seem, and smarter than you think."

This craft was inspired by Amanda Formaro at craftsbyamanda.com. To see examples of Kindness Rocks and for quotes and words you can use on your own rocks, visit thewellcraftedmom.com/coaching-craft.

Part 3

FLY

Find Fun
Live by Heart
Your Turn

"Eagles and hummingbirds, butterflies and bees know—
there is more than one way to fly."

Amy Tiemann

Chapter Ten

Find Fun

*"...when you sense a faint potentiality for happiness after such
dark times you must grab onto the ankles of that happiness and
not let go until it drags you face-first out of the dirt—this is not
selfishness, but obligation. You were given life; it is your duty
(and also your entitlement as a human being) to find something
beautiful within life, no matter how slight."*
Elizabeth Gilbert

I had forgotten how to have fun. I enjoyed spending time with my
husband and my children and loved how the three of them knew exactly
how to make me laugh (usually with a fart joke), but I didn't have time
for the hobbies I once enjoyed. My art supplies sat in a cabinet, jewelry-

making materials were stacked up on shelves in the garage, my dance shoes were retired to the back of the closet. I couldn't find the time for an art workshop or dance class. It was too much trouble to pull out all the art supplies, set up projects on the kitchen table during nap time, and then shove it all away at the first sounds of children stirring from their naps. If they even napped. It wasn't worth the effort: my time alone was too unpredictable, I was too tired, and my mommy cup overflowed with chores and responsibilities.

The only time I was creative was when I did arts and crafts with my sons. I learned the Buddhist principle of non-attachment when my boys and I finger-painted, drew with crayons, or glued stuff together. They liked to "improve" my creations with their own artwork, adding stickers, scribbles, and streaks. It was fun sharing my love of art with them, but the process wasn't really artistic, and it left me thirsty for more.

I needed some creative juice just for me.

With the help of our couples counselor, my husband and I negotiated an arrangement: once a week he would take the boys to their schools and then work from a cafe instead of at home, creating quiet time for my introverted self and giving uninterrupted creative time to my artist within. Each Wednesday, he would load the kids in the car and I would wave goodbye from the doorway, blowing kisses and smiling, but wishing he would back out of the driveway more quickly. *Goodbye! Goodbye, again! Another kiss!* Finally, I would lock the front door, nestle into my favorite spot on the couch, and pick up my sketchbook or journal.

I spent the first month of my time alone sleeping.

That time felt wasted, like I had paid for a seat at a Broadway musical and then waited out the entire show in the lobby. But every Wednesday it was the same: once my house was quiet and the cat was settled on the blanket covering my feet, I couldn't keep my eyes open.

After a month of resting, I entered a different phase. Now, after my husband and the kids left, I had to resist the pull of the undone chores, previously ignored. There were piles of toys that hadn't made it into the baskets, there were sticky floors, dirty dishes, and large piles of laundry. I keenly felt the tug of war between my inner Mean Manager and Kind Caretaker. The manager said I needed to pay for my special time alone by finishing a chunk of chores, then I could relax with whatever time was left over. The caretaker responded by gently insisting rest was best.

When Wednesday mornings rolled around, I'd compromise by putting one load of laundry in the washing machine, transferring the dishes in the sink to the dishwasher, and organizing the toys in the baskets. But one chore would lead to another, my time alone would shrink, and the morning would become like all the rest—filled with what needed to be done but not what I needed for myself.

I knew it was my responsibility to create time for myself and fill it with what nourished me, with activities, daydreams, and whatever else replenished my energetic pantry so I had the desire and incentive to give back to my family, my clients, and to my other obligations. I knew fun and pleasure resided somewhere between the Mean Manager's to do list and the Kind Caretaker's spot on the couch. The playful me was still there after two kids, but buried beneath scattered toys, dirty laundry, and cleaning supplies.

Mihaly Csikszentmihalyi, Distinguished Professor of Psychology and Management at Claremont Graduate University and author of the book *Flow: The Psychology of Optimal Experience*, says people tend to feel anxious when they don't have a clear goal or when they are alone. Under these circumstances, the brain's built-in negativity bias stands up and starts searching for problems. People ease this anxiety by filling their time with watching television, browsing the Internet, reading romance novels, or with other passive leisure activities. "These are quick ways to reduce chaos in consciousness in the short run, but usually the only residue they leave behind is a feeling of listless dissatisfaction."

That's how I felt, exactly. Listless. Dissatisfied. Empty. Like I had been giving and giving and now my essential cupboard was bare and nothing I was doing was restocking the shelves.

This may be how you're feeling, too. It may be why it feels like not enough, like a waste, when you spend your "me time" scrolling through social media, watching television, or reading the latest chick lit novel once the kids are in bed and your husband is focused on his computer. Like your time spent with yourself wasn't well spent.

Csikszentmihalyi writes: "To make the best use of free time, one needs to devote as much ingenuity and attention to it as one would to one's job. Active leisure that helps a person grow does not come easy."

I really wanted the solution to be easy. As easy as putting on my running shoes and heading out for a five-mile run. But just as my out-of-shape body couldn't possibly run for five miles, my out-of-shape mind couldn't seem to find a way to have fun.

"The gap between where you presently are and where you want to be is telling you that there is a life force in you that wants to come out and express itself. It is pointing you toward a fuller, more vital life," says Anat Baniel in her book *Move Into Life: The Nine Essentials for Lifelong Vitality.* "To bring vitality into our lives, our brains need to be at the ready–to amplify, intensify, and create new patterns while strengthening the ones that already work for us. And that's where enthusiasm comes in."

Baniel writes that children are naturally excited and find fun all around them. They are ready for play and it comes spontaneously and naturally. But predictable grown-up routines don't usually offer reasons to feel exuberant. Baniel recommends replacing childlike excitement with adult enthusiasm. "Enthusiasm does for the adult brain what excitement does for the child's brain," writes Baniel. "While the child's excitement is triggered by the new, and mostly from events outside of her, adult enthusiasm is initiated from within and is a set of intentionally applied skills."

Baniel sees enthusiasm as a generator, the voluntary power behind saying "Yes, please," to life. Enthusiasm invigorates your life with playfulness. You can choose to focus your enthusiasm on any part of your life you want to change for the better, making room for intentional, purposeful play.

The Purpose of Play

Active leisure, which could also be called *play*, is hard to define. Stuart Brown, M.D., author of the book *Play: How It Shapes the Brain, Opens the Imagination, and Invigorates the Soul*, narrows the definition of play down to seven different qualities: play is voluntary, unexpected, has no obvious purpose, creates enjoyment, eases self-consciousness, distracts from the passing of time, and is difficult to stop once started.

The benefits of play are many. Playfulness expert Lynn A. Barnett, an associate professor at the University of Illinois, has found that people who are more playful manage their stress better than their more serious counterparts. "People who are playful don't run away from stress, they deal with it–they don't do avoidance," Barnett said in a *Boston Globe* article. Being playful improves creativity, intrinsic motivation, job satisfaction, even quality of life.

Playing with your children can certainly reduce stress. But when you're with your children, your playfulness has a grown-up quality to it–you still need to be in charge when you're with your children. The challenge is finding fun just for you.

That's what I was determined to uncover. When I went searching, I discovered that finding fun for grown-ups follows a few basic principles:

Look back. Journey back to your childhood and remember how you played when you were young. Make a list of what delighted you when you were little and recreate elements of your childhood play in your grown-up life. If you can, go back to being eight years old, a magical time when you were old enough to make a few choices about how you wanted to spend your time and young enough to not be fully locked into the expectations of others. Were you driven to win the neighborhood kickball game? Did you enjoy scribbling and drawing on every piece of paper? Did you love to climb as high as you could in the big tree in your backyard, reveling in the tingly sensation of danger?

"Remember and *feel* that emotion and hold on to it, because that's what's going to save you," writes Stuart Brown in *Play*. "The memory of that emotion is going to be the life raft that keeps you from drowning. It can be the rope that lifts you out of your play-deficient well."

Move your body. Exercise has many proven benefits. It can improve your health, lengthen your life, and raise your spirits. But if exercise doesn't feel like fun, it won't feed your soul. After trying to build a consistent exercise routine and repeatedly failing, I resolved to exercise by doing only what felt like fun. I started tap dancing again. I enrolled in an aerobics class that delightfully and unexpectedly included hip hop choreography (and the center where I took the class provided childcare for a small fee). I hiked with friends and family. I mapped out a walk/run route that took me through the "hidden parks" in my neighborhood, and I stopped tracking time, speed, and distance. Since implementing my fun movement plan, I've consistently exercised three times every week, and often more. I'm happier, more fit, and my soul feels full.

Be silly. Becoming a parent gives you permission to play again, to be light-hearted and creative. When you wrestle, tickle, and laugh with your child, you become more childlike, which can nourish you emotionally. That same playfulness can be taken into your play time outside of parenthood when you try new things, like taking a class in anything from coding to ceramics. "Play is *exploration*," writes Stuart Brown in *Play*. "Which means that you will be going places where you haven't been before."

Do more, have less. A research study cleverly titled *Waiting for Merlot: Anticipatory Consumption of Experiential and Material Purchases* discovered when people spend money on activities their happiness lasts longer than when they spend money on items. Even the anticipation of an experience, like a trip to the beach, art class, or date night with your spouse, creates more enthusiasm than waiting for your online purchase to arrive.

Waiting for Merlot researcher Thomas Gilovich's work suggests experiences tend to lead to more happiness because people are less likely to measure the value of their experiences by comparing them to other peoples' experiences, unlike the way people compare possessions. In his study *To Do or To Have? That is the Question*, Gilovich discovered that when research participants evaluated their experiential and material purchases, they were much more likely to say their money was well spent on activities and less so on physical goods.

Find flow. Flow is play with a mindful focus. It's that time when you're engaged in an activity, whether it's a sport, artistic endeavor, or even a work project, and you lose all sense of time. Csikszentmihaly talked with people throughout the world and found the sensation of flow is similar whether it's found while surfing a wave or building a birdhouse, and is the same despite differences in age, culture, or gender.

"Human beings feel best in flow, when they are fully involved in meeting a challenge, solving a problem, discovering something new," writes Csikszentmihaly in his book *Finding Flow: The Psychology of Engagement in Everyday Life*. "Most activities that produce flow also have clear goals, clear rules, immediate feedback–a set of external demands that focuses our attention and makes demands on our skills."

If you look closely at your activities that create the feeling of flow, you may be surprised to see the presence of these external parameters: clear goals, clear rules, and immediate feedback. With scrapbooking, your goal is to create a page or two in your scrapbook to capture a pleasurable experience; the rules are to use your paper, photographs, stickers, and tape to make pages that fit within your book; and the immediate feedback is your sense of accomplishment as your ideas are turned into beautiful creations. Whether you're swimming, dancing, writing, painting, or engaged in any challenging activity, look for projects that build on these three elements to help set the foundation for flow.

Flow, also called *engagement*, is one of the five essential elements of well-being, according to a field of study called Positive Psychology (the other elements in Positive Psychology's model of well-being are positive experiences, relationships, meaning, and achievement). But the state of flow can be hard for moms to find; two of the eight major components of flow listed by Csikszentmihalyi in a Global Learning Communities paper—working with tasks you have a chance of completing and being able to concentrate on what you're doing—are often unattainable for moms with small children. Your kids seem to intuitively know (and want to interrupt) when you're not 100 percent emotionally, mentally, and physically available to satisfy their needs. The importance of flow experiences for happiness increases the necessity of setting aside time for yourself and protecting it from interruption or dissolution.

For me, once I wrestled free from the workaholic demands of my inner Mean Manager and eased out of the arms of my permissive Kind Caretaker, I started making jewelry again. I bought interlocking boxes to organize my tools and supplies. I set up my creative station on an old baking sheet that could be easily–albeit sometimes reluctantly–moved back to the garage once my creative time was over. My once-a-week time alone became the sustenance I looked forward to all week. At the table, with the jewelry supplies, the torch, and the tools, the old me and the mommy me found our fun, together.

Practical Advice – The Doorway between Work and Play

There are always parts of life that don't feel like fun. Tasks you don't want to do, responsibilities that feel obligatory, perhaps even a job you dread. But bringing play into your work is possible, even if you have a job you dislike. "Play can transform work. It can bring back excitement and newness to the job," writes Stuart Brown in his book *Play*. "Play helps us deal with difficulties, provides a sense of expansiveness, promotes mastery of our craft, and is an essential part of the creative process. Most important, true play that comes from our own inner needs and desires is the only path to finding lasting joy and satisfaction in our work. In the long run, work does not work without play."

But how do you integrate play into what feels like work? One way is to identify the aspects of your job—whether it's a stay-at-home mommy job or an out-in-the-world career—that feel more like fun and the parts that feel more like, well, work. At home, fun might be wrestling with your kids, researching redecorating ideas, or following a new recipe to prepare a delicious meal. At work, play could be anything that lights you up, whether it's meeting with your team or writing marketing copy. "Part of virtually any job has the possibility to be as enjoyable, as enthralling and creative as when we were kids building sand castles on the beach or flying a kite we created out of sticks, newspaper, and string," writes Stuart Brown. "The joy has to find its way to us, and us to it."

Another way to integrate play into work is to intentionally manage the shifts between play and work. Paul Dolan in his book *Happiness by Design: Change What You Do Not How You Think*, describes a process that can help bring out the most joy in your job. Start by spending time on a pleasurable project. When happiness begins to wane, shift your activity to a more purposeful—and less fun—activity. At home, this would be like stopping a craft project when you get frustrated and shifting your attention to cleaning up the kitchen. Or, at your job, once your attention begins to wander when you're working on an enjoyable and creative project, start in on your expense report. Then, when your focus ebbs on the more mundane activity, return to what was pleasurable, either the first project or something else. This focuses your attention and prevents your brain from becoming habituated to the pleasurable activity, which can make it commonplace.

You can also bring a playful attitude to what feels like work, easing the negative pull on your mood. "Work matters, but we often allow day-to-day events at work to give us more anxiety than they are worth," writes Stuart Brown. "Getting oneself into a play state, however, masks the urgent purposefulness and associated anxiety of work, increasing efficiency and productivity." Review your Time Well Spent list from Chapter Five to find ways to be playful while you work. You might listen to music, decorate your workspace (or the front of your refrigerator if you're at home) with pictures of yourself and friends engaged in fun activities, or plan a fun lunchtime outing to build your anticipation throughout the morning.

If your work is beyond redemption and there's no aspect of it that feels like fun, it becomes even more important that you include opportunities for play, pleasure, and flow in your free time. "Luckily the world is absolutely full of interesting things to do," writes Cskiszentmihalyi. "Only lack of imagination, or lack of energy, stand in the way."

Coaching + Craft – Light-as-a-Feather Stir Sticks

"Play is the stick that stirs the drink. It is the basis of all art, games, books, sports, movies, fashion, fun, and wonder–in short, the basis of what we think of as civilization," writes Stuart Brown. This chapter's project is a reminder for you to create your own fun. By creating the stick that stirs your cocktails or mocktails, you'll have a reminder to create time for your own fun.

Coaching + Craft Project Supplies

- Feathers of different sizes, about one-half inch to two inches in length
- Bamboo skewers or plastic swizzle sticks
- Narrow ribbon in whatever color you prefer
- Scissors
- Glue gun (preferred) or glue

Group your feathers by size so you have four categories of feathers, from largest to smallest. Start with a feather from the big pile and glue the bottom edge of the quill to the top edge of the swizzle stick or skewer (not the pointy end). Select a feather from the next category of feathers, one size smaller, and glue it onto the skewer, across from the first feather. Continue gluing feathers to the skewer until you have four of them attached.

Place a small bead of glue on the skewer near the bottom of the quills and attach the end of your ribbon. Twist the ribbon around the skewer to cover the bottom part of the feathers. Finish with another bead of glue and cut off the excess ribbon. Cut the bottom of the skewers so they match the height of your drink glasses.

When you play, your responsibilities and obligations can feel as light as a feather and your troubles can float away. "I don't think it is too much to say that play can save your life," writes Stuart Brown. "It certainly has salvaged mine."

This chapter's Coaching + Craft project is from Frugal Living Adventures. You can see examples of what others moms have created in our workshops and get ideas of what you can create at thewellcraftedmom.com/coaching-craft.

Chapter Eleven

Live by Heart

*"As you learn to live by heart, every choice you make will become
another way of telling your story, calling your tribe, and liberating
not only your heart but the hearts of others.
This is the very definition of love."*
Martha Beck

I had been following a blog written by a writer named Annie
O'Shaughnessy for several years, delighted each time I saw an email
with her latest post in my inbox. When I first discovered her work, she
was married to an artist, and their newsletters were a blend of his soft
watercolors and her strong words. They parted and she began anew,
starting a nonprofit where she wrote, shared the art of others, and led

retreats called *Reconnecting with Our Wild Souls*. One day she sent an email announcing a three-day retreat on the West Coast, saying this one would be her last.

I felt a tug in my heart that I dimly recognized. It was the first time I had felt desire in a while. Even before becoming a mom, I had felt disconnected, like there was an insurmountable gap between what I deeply wanted and what was possible; it was far easier to stop wishing for more than to take a leap toward what was perpetually out of reach. I hesitated each time I stood on the rim of possibility–starting a new business, writing a book, even holding the simple wish to find time to be creative–held back by a suspicion that I wasn't good enough or smart enough to manifest my desires.

This wasn't a new pattern; I had spent a lifetime playing small, elaborately covering up who I really was, agreeing when I really didn't, feeling lonely even when I was surrounded by people. Annie's retreat sounded like the perfect way to fix this, to fix me. My husband confidently assured me that a long weekend without me would be a breeze (which turned out to be true, evidenced by a spectacularly clean house and happy boys when I returned), so I signed up.

Annie's retreat was held in Point Reyes National Seashore, about an hour north of San Francisco, at the Commonweal Retreat Center, which sits on a bluff above the shore of the Pacific Ocean. I arrived nervously early on that first day, the first car in the parking area. The retreat house was unlocked and empty and I explored the bedrooms, finally choosing one upstairs in the corner, with windows looking out into the cypress trees. I opened the windows to let in the foggy ocean air and sat on the bed, thinking about my hopes for the retreat, about how I wanted to be over the weekend.

Our group came together in the large living room on that first evening. Annie distributed a spiral wire-bound book for each of us that included a schedule, intentions, an explanation of how Annie leads her circles. As we introduced ourselves, we passed around a talking stone, a palm-sized, flat, smooth rock with a spiraling ink drawing on it. Whoever had the stone spoke without interruption.

On that first evening, Annie suggested that we invite our biggest fear into the room, acknowledge it, honor it, and then ask it to leave. I thought about my fear of being seen for who I truly was, worn like a snake, its unwelcome heaviness coiled around me, pinning my arms, its thick tail against my lips, a familiar reminder to stay small, be quiet. How do you ask something to leave that's so firmly entwined with who you are? It was like politely asking an anaconda to let go.

I felt the snake limiting my movements when the group danced to music, quieting my voice when I thought of something to say, squeezing my ribcage whenever I held the talking stone. I was so used to squirming, hiding, and pretending, my self-consciousness felt like an inseparable second skin. But this weekend felt different: I wanted the snake to let go.

It was uncomfortable to wrestle with my deeply lodged beliefs in front of an audience of strangers, even compassionate ones. Despite my discomfort—or perhaps because of it—Annie's *Wild Souls* retreat loosened the skin of my self-consciousness. The act of being vulnerable, even in small pieces, created an opening. A crack. Underneath, I saw how flawed I was, but I also saw faint beauty, a hint of what I could be in this world.

Annie asked each of us create our own soul declaration, a ritual for our healing that we would share with the group on the last full day of the retreat. I struggled to come up with a ritual, knowing at some level that I couldn't think my way through this, that the answer had to come from a deeper part of me.

I went for a run, took a long solitary walk to the beach and collected rocks, sat on a stone bench overlooking a meadow and the ocean in the distance. Sitting on the bench, I wrote down what I wanted to hear from others, what would ease the tightness in my throat, the constriction in my torso, the hesitancy in my voice. I wrote messages to myself on torn slips of paper, gathered them together, and placed them in a cup. My soul declaration with the group was a quiet ritual of people selecting a slip and whispering the words to me that I needed to hear: *you are lovable, you are loved, you are forgiven.*

"Our Soul's longing to be whole is so strong it leads us to the areas in us that need tending," writes Annie in her blog, now posted on her website at truenatureguidance.com. "We cannot dictate the unfolding."

Unfolding meant loving all of my bits and pieces, even the parts that don't go together, like my fierce protectiveness of my "me time" and my desire to give to others. Or my bad temper and my patience. Inherent laziness and picky perfectionism. Healing came from going home and slowly showing more and more of the parts of me and my past that I had shrouded in shame to my husband, close friends, and then a wider and wider circle of people I trusted. Saying in words and actions, "I don't like this about me but …" and mostly receiving loving acceptance, wry recognition, or a blasé attitude like "Why is that a thing?"

The crack in my restrictive second skin became deeper and wider, running the whole length of me, until I moved on, leaving the old husk behind.

Authenticity

Showing up fully is the practice of authenticity. "Authenticity is a collection of choices that we have to make every day," writes Brené Brown in *The Gifts of Imperfection*. "It's about the choice to show up and be real. The choice to be honest. The choice to let our true selves be seen."

But being seen is an uncomfortable place to be. You may believe that your second skin helps you to blend in with everything (and everybody) but when you finally stop racing around and filling your days with being busy, you find yourself asking the question "Is this all there is?" Relationships suffer when you don't speak your piece, say what matters, and be yourself. When you aren't authentic, you suffer because the ideas and dreams that you push under the carpet don't go away. Instead they turn ugly and become envy, jealousy, resentment, anger, even depression.

Your second skin may feel so familiar that you don't notice it anymore, not really, but there's a deep longing for your life to feel different. Showing up as yourself is a moment-by-moment act of being transparent, authentic, and open. Author Martha Beck abbreviates these qualities to TAO, a word that means *the way* in Buddhist thought—the way towards living a lighter life, without the heavy snake on your shoulders.

Being TAO—what Martha Beck defines as transparent, authentic, and open—takes practice, because to do so, you must override messages from your past that may be deeply ingrained, like the Mean Manager's voice that says "You're getting too big for your britches." It takes courage to be TAO because, in doing so, you're choosing to break the social rules of *stay quiet, don't make a fuss*. You run the risk of being rejected. Aligning your behavior with your values—and even knowing what your values are—involves listening and trusting yourself at your deepest level.

"Authenticity demands wholehearted living and loving, even when it's hard, even when we're wrestling with the shame and fear of not being good enough, and especially when the joy is so intense that we're afraid to let ourselves feel it," writes Brené Brown. "Mindfully practicing authenticity during our most soul-searching struggles is how we invite grace, joy, and gratitude into our lives."

Meeting Your True Self

Each one of us has a deep, fundamental nature within, what Annie O'Shaughnessy calls *the soul*, what author Martha Beck calls *the essential self*. "It's the basic you, stripped of options and special features," writes Martha Beck in *Finding Your Own North Star*. "It is 'essential' in two ways: first, it is the essence of your personality, and second, you absolutely need it to find your North Star."

You listen to your essential self by tuning in to the sensations in your body. Just like when you're nervous about walking through a dark, empty parking garage and the hair stands up on the back of your neck as a reminder to be alert, pay attention, get out your keys, and get to the car, your essential self lets you know when you're walking toward happiness or headed toward danger or despair. Your essential self talks to you when your muscles tighten up, speaks when your breath gets shallow, and shouts at you with chronic pain. You can also feel your essential self in the relaxed bliss of holding a sleeping baby in your arms. It's the elation you experience throughout your body when you've met an important, self-directed goal, whether it's a project at work or reaching the top of a hill on a hike. It's the inner navigational magnet that pulls you toward the rich ore of a fulfilling life.

In contrast, the social self responds to the rules and expectations of your family, culture, and peers. Your social self is the part you polish by adjusting your behavior to blend in, fudging the truth a little so that you measure up, and following the rules even when it doesn't feel good.

When you start paying attention to the little clues, like how the knot in your throat eases up when you're with good friends, or how you forget about the ringing in your ears when you're focused on a creative project, or how you can take a full breath when you're sketching in your notebook, you can more easily follow the path to what feels like a challenging, happy, fulfilling life.

Try it right now. Think of a moment in your past when you were happy, whether you were sitting on a warm beach with your toes in the sand, or laughingly racing with your daughter and letting her win, or watching your children sleep. It can be just a snippet of time. Bring this one memory into full detail by recalling the moment with all of your senses: the color of the sea, the texture of the blanket, the sound of your daughter giggling, or her relaxed breath while she slept. Then notice what happens in your body when your essential self is happy with where you are. Do you feel calmer? Where do you notice peace in your body? Are your muscles more relaxed? Do you feel lighter, like a burden's been lifted?

You can go the other way with this exercise by focusing on a negative experience and paying attention to how it affects your body, but you probably already know what that feels like: tightness in your throat, like you've swallowed rocks; upset in your stomach that feels like small, angry animals in your tummy; tension in your shoulders as if you're carrying the weight of the world.

This is your body's way of passing along the messages that are deeply held at your core, the messages from your essential self. You can bring this awareness into your everyday life, using any moment as a way to check your course, by asking yourself *Does this choice feel light and right or dark and down?* and making your choices accordingly. "The only map of your right life is written on your soul at its most peaceful, and the only sure compass is your heart at its most open," writes Martha Beck.

Ideally, your social self and essential self work hand in hand for you to meet your desires, achieve your goals, and lead a fulfilling life. For example, if your essential self yearns to be outdoors, the social self researches good hikes for families, loads the kids in the car, and heads out for an afternoon spent in nature. Your essential self knows what feeds your soul, nourishes your happiness, and allows joy to grow, and your social self is highly capable of working out the logistics. But many people have stopped listening to the essential self because the soul's instructions are often indistinct, there are too many other responsibilities, and there's no time to be creative, to take care of yourself, or to play.

The social self ends up in charge. But this part of you only knows what's worked for other people–the "tried and true" way to inner peace. Not *your* way, not *your* path. When the social self is in the driver's seat, you're often led to frustration, depression, anxiety, and despair.

When you give your essential self the keys, you realize that peace already permeates the air, like a breeze that streams through windows opened wide. As one mother so clearly pointed out in one of my workshops, "Sometimes knowing which way to go isn't about looking to the future; it can be about seeing what's right in front of you."

Practical Advice – Finding the Way

In my training program to become a life coach, all the students were encouraged to find a "buddy," another person in the program with whom we could practice the concepts and tools we were learning. While still on the first training call, I scrolled through the coach trainee bios, looking for a buddy who was in my time zone and who had made similar life choices as me, like motherhood and self-employment. I narrowed my choice down to one woman, Christy Miller. She looked ideal: a mom of two boys, just like me; a freelance graphic designer; a California resident. Toward the end of the training call, I copied and pasted her address into a new email, preparing to send a request and introduce myself after class. Just before the call ended, an email from her was in my inbox, titled *Want to be my Martha Beck buddy?*

Over the next nine months of the training program, we spent many hours together on the phone, practicing techniques and tools. To obtain the full benefits of the coaching program, we each had to be vulnerable, sharing our stories, putting the critical voices of our self-conscious social selves on mute.

Our relationship should have felt forced. It should have been awkward and uncomfortable, like a little seat of nails every Monday morning when it was my turn to be coached by Christy.

It was actually a relief.

I couldn't remember ever starting a friendship off this way–because that's what it ended up becoming, a true friendship. It was like inviting a stranger off the street into the messiness of the most private room in my house. My perfectionism–mostly lapsed, although I still bowed to its tyrannical power more than I liked–pushed me to want to do well, which meant being the ideal client for my coaching buddy. So, instead of shoving my personal struggles under the bed like I would normally do in the presence of a new acquaintance, I left them littered on the floor, even pointing them out so Christy wouldn't miss them: *Here's where I'm not making it as a mom. Over there is my pile of regrets. Careful! Don't trip over my temper.*

Christy was equally honest in her practice coaching sessions with me. I felt tenderhearted toward what she claimed were failings, like they were real, fluffy bunnies under her psychological bed. Christy's vulnerability made her more lovable, complex, and cherished.

Since completing my life coach training, I have felt the same way about my coaching clients, my family and friends, my support group of eight other life coaches who talk every month and meet in person twice a year: the more they share their struggles, faults, and failings, the more beloved they become to me.

I wish I could say that the process of learning to be transparent, authentic, and open is easy. Frankly, it's hard, especially at the beginning when fear pulls the second skin tight. But the rewards of living true to your essential self are great: deep relationships, enlightened creativity, and rich joy.

Here's where you begin:

Build your safety net. Develop a relationship with a trusted backup person with whom you can be vulnerable and confide in if things don't go well at first. This could be a friend, family member, psychologist, or life coach.

Start where you can bear to fail. Putting yourself on the line to be completely TAO is scary. To minimize your fear, start with small risks, like sharing a disappointment with a close friend or asking for advice about a minor issue from someone you don't know very well yet. Once you take the first tiny step toward greater intimacy, wait to see if your bid is reciprocated. If it isn't, check in with your essential self to know whether to try again. When your first venture into vulnerability goes well, take another step, and then another after that. Big change grows from small seeds planted well.

Choose what you put on the table. Understand that when things don't go well it's not a reflection of your essential self. "When you get to a place where you understand that love and belonging, your worthiness, is a birthright and not something you have to earn, anything is possible," says Brené Brown, quoted in an article on the ted.com blog. "Your raise can be on the table, your promotion can be on the table, your title can be on the table, your grades can be on the table. But keep your worthiness for love and belonging off the table. And then ironically everything else just takes care of itself."

To be authentic, you need to get under your skin, to not only see your beauty that rises like steam from the brightness of your soul, but to ease free from the belief that at your core there is something unlovable about you. Listening to your essential self in the beginning is like listening to the whispered voices of compassionate strangers who can see your soul through the translucent skin of your constricted social self. Listen as they quietly repeat what's true: *you are lovable, you are loved, you are forgiven.*

Coaching + Craft – Coming Full Circle

Mandalas are detailed circular designs, typically with a center point, used in many spiritual traditions as a tool for focusing attention, bringing harmony, enhancing creativity, and calling in an inner spiritual force. Psychologist Carl Jung said that a mandala symbolizes "a safe refuge of inner reconciliation and wholeness." Creating a mandala–or even coloring a mandala design downloaded from the Internet–gives you the opportunity to "pay attention on purpose," reducing ruminating thoughts, anxiety, even physical discomfort.

This chapter's project is about decorating a plate with a mandala design to use as a reminder to be more mindful in your everyday life. By creating and using your mandala as part of a mindfulness practice, you learn to pay attention and live by your heart.

If this project feels too big or if obtaining the supplies is a challenge, you can modify the activity and obtain the same benefits by using colored pencils or markers to make your mandala on a circular piece of paper.

Coaching + Craft Project Supplies

- White or light-colored plate (a thrift store or dollar store is a great resource)
- Rubbing alcohol
- Cotton rags (for cleaning the plate)
- Cotton swabs (for wiping away mistakes)
- Pencil
- Compass for drawing circles (optional)
- Rubber stamps
- Stazon alcohol ink pads
- Oil-based Sharpie pens

Clean the plate with rubbing alcohol and let it dry completely.

For the mandala design for your plate, you can copy designs from mandala coloring pages from the Internet, check thewellcraftedmom.

com/coaching-craft to see what other moms have made in Coaching +
Craft gatherings, or design your own mandala.

To draw your own mandala, use a pencil to make one small circle
in the center of the plate and then larger circles in rings around the
center towards the outside of the plate. Using stamps, ink pads, and
pens, make patterns along the circles that please your inner essential
self. Your mandala can be as detailed or as simple as you like, and may
include images, words, and as many or few colors as you choose. If you
want to make changes, you can wipe off what you don't want with a little
alcohol on a cotton swab, remembering to let the alcohol dry before
drawing in that area again.

Put the plate–or plates, if you're making more than one–in the oven
and heat it to 400 degrees. Bake the plate for 30 minutes, turn the oven
off, and let the plate sit in the oven until the plate is cool enough to
touch. If you remove it too soon, the plate might crack. Hand wash
your mandala plate to protect the design. Your plate is best used for
decorative purposes only.

To use your mandala as a meditative tool, set it where you can see it
clearly. Focus your attention on your breath and allow your focus to stay
with your mandala. When your attention wanders, gently bring it back
to focus on the mandala.

Simply creating your mandala is a powerful healing tool. As you draw
and paint your mandala, you'll be able to circle back to the voice of your
essential self, an inner guide directing you toward greater fulfillment.

For a while, Carl Jung drew a mandala daily. "I guarded them like precious
pearls," he wrote. "It became increasingly plain to me that the mandala is the
center. It is the exponent of all paths. It is the path to the center."

This chapter's craft idea was inspired by Natasha at The
Artisan Life and Renee at Bolton House. See examples of mandalas
that moms have made during Coaching + Craft gatherings at
thewellcraftedmom.com/coaching-craft.

Chapter Twelve

Your Turn

"You were born with wings."
Rumi

It was late October. My husband, the boys, and I were spending a few days in Pacific Grove, a small town in Northern California, next to Monterey, not far from the aquarium. We had found an inexpensive hotel, tucked away on a residential street, which looked like it hadn't been updated for several decades. Its dusty neglect was redeemed by windows that spanned two walls, one overlooking a giant cypress to the north, and the other opening to the edge of the monarch butterflies' overwintering spot to the west.

My husband and I unloaded the car, trudging up and down the narrow staircase, followed closely by the two boys who were antsy from being cooped up on the drive. Once we had unloaded suitcases, backpacks, toys, and other paraphernalia in our two-room suite, we walked to the nearby Monarch Butterfly Sanctuary.

The Monarch Butterfly Sanctuary in Pacific Grove is one of many places in California and Mexico where monarch butterflies migrate each fall. We were visiting during the early overwintering season; butterflies had just begun congregating in the grove a week or so earlier. Informational signs and interactive educational displays lined the shady winding path that wound through the wooded grove. Our younger son bolted down the path with my husband in pursuit and our older boy stayed behind with me.

"Look!" My son pointed up into a tree where butterflies flew high above us, hundreds of them floating, landing on branches, then rising into the air again. He reached for my hand and we stood there together, watching the monarchs fluttering in and out of the leaves of the eucalyptus trees. I felt a fluttering in my heart, too, and smiled in recognition: happiness had found its way home to me.

I was a different mom now than the one who walked with my husband into the couples counselor's office for our first appointment nearly two years ago: defeated, raw, and ready to run. I was no longer the insecure mother who stood at the precipice between what I wanted and what I thought I deserved. I wasn't a woman who looked in the mirror and saw only a failure.

I had wished long and hard for life to be easier, like it had been in my BC (before children) life. I had longed for a magical time shift that would bring back freedom I could fritter away like bread crumbs fed to pigeons in the park. But through the hard work of becoming the mother I wanted to be, I'd realized that what I longed for was really only crumbs, not enough to sustain the stronger, more insightful, and loving person who had emerged. My heart could now hold so much more than it had held before I became a mom.

I had created a new kind of happiness by learning how to say no to what didn't feed my soul or my family, asking for what I wanted, and embracing what I couldn't change. I felt like the butterflies in the trees: resilient; connected to a community; and possessing a deep wisdom that led me to an inner peace that felt like home, even though it was a place I'd never been before. I had crafted a happier life from scratch with new tools earned the hard way, a bigger perspective gleaned from eye-opening experiences, genuine love for my husband and children, and tender affection for myself.

Little by little, I had crafted my own wings.

Growing Wings

The kindergarteners who had watched the caterpillars transform into chrysalises eagerly waited for butterflies to emerge. One day while I was volunteering in the classroom, a butterfly crawled from its chrysalis, which was fastened to the top of the mesh enclosure by caterpillar silk. The kids crowded around to see the butterfly, its wings crumpled and wet. As the butterfly hung from the empty chrysalis, it slowly and rhythmically pumped its wings which grew larger, preparing the butterfly for flight.

Like the butterfly, you, too, were born with wings. They may not be quite ready for flight, but even small efforts will increase your strength so you can fly. The time to start is now. "Don't wait until all the conditions are perfect for you to begin," writes author Alan Cohen. "Beginning makes the conditions perfect."

These are the qualities that will build your strength so you can fly: courage, hope, hard work, and curiosity.

How brave can you be? Crafting the life you want takes courage, but you can build your bravery one moment at a time. "We do not have to become heroes overnight," wrote Eleanor Roosevelt. "Just a step at a time, meeting each thing that comes up, seeing it is not as dreadful as it appeared, discovering we have the strength to stare it down." You can be brave when you ask for advice from a mom you don't know so well, negotiate more time to invest in self-care and the pursuit of your dreams, or engage authentically even when what you believe isn't popular.

Professor and author Salvatore R. Maddi calls this resilience *hardiness*. "Hardiness is a combination of attitudes that provides the courage and motivation to do the hard, strategic work of turning stressful circumstances from potential disasters into growth opportunities," he writes in "Hardiness: The Courage to Grow from Stresses," an article published in the *Journal of Positive Psychology*. Maddi, who developed a hardiness training program that gives people tools and resources for handling stress and adversity, says that hardy attitudes consist of three C's: commitment to your goals, control over your environment, and challenging yourself.

Commitment to your goals is when you say no when everyone expects you to step up and take on another volunteer project at your child's school. Control over your environment is when you take the first step toward repairing your relationship with your spouse by giving him an unexpected kiss before he leaves for work. Challenging yourself happens when you ask a new mom out to coffee to begin building a foundation for a new friendship.

Every day you can renew your commitment to being more brave. "Courage doesn't always roar," writes artist and writer Mary Anne Radmacher. "Sometimes courage is the little voice at the end of the day that says *I'll try again tomorrow.*"

Hold on to hope. Research has shown hope is a skill you can learn. "A true and deep experience of hope can also bring a richer and more lasting form of happiness, beyond superficial or fleeting moments of 'hurried excitement,'" writes Anthony Scioli in *Hope in the Age of Anxiety*.

"In contrast, a well-founded hope that bridges the past, present, and future can ensure joy, happiness, and pleasure, for today and tomorrow as well as next year and beyond."

It's easy to lose hope if you believe every thought you think. Your brain is programmed to continually search for proof that supports negative thoughts. To build hope, you can examine the story you're telling yourself and question it from the Kind Caretaker's perspective, not the Mean Manager's doom and gloom mindset.

Byron Katie, author of *Loving What Is: Four Questions That Can Change Your Life*, helps people become more aware of the Mean Manager's role in creating hopelessness with a process of four questions, the first question being "Is it true?" Just by questioning your thoughts and mistrusting faulty evidence, you can be more hopeful for a happier future.

Hope is knowing that you will create the time to care for yourself despite the many demands on your time and energy. Hope is when you build a plan to nurture your creativity and discover your own next steps for your life and your career. Hope keeps you headed toward what you want but aren't sure you will ever hold. "Hope begins in the dark, the stubborn hope that if you just show up and try to do the right thing, the dawn will come," writes author Anne Lamott. "You wait and watch and work: you don't give up."

Make the effort. In the same way a butterfly must pump its wings to get strong enough to fly, applying effort is what will give you the strength to find your own sanctuary. As Carol Dweck, Stanford University professor and author of *Mindset: The New Psychology of Success* writes: "No matter what your ability is, effort is what ignites that ability and turns it into accomplishment."

Occasionally, good fortune lands in your lap, unforeseen and full of promise. Reaching your goals, however, often takes work: the labyrinthine progress of your Elephant's emotions and Rider's reasons, the ongoing negotiation between what your essential self desires and what your social self can comfortably permit, your Kind Caretaker's recommendations for rest in opposition to your Mean Manager's list of chores.

Putting in the effort means that every moment is one you can use toward building your strength and taking another step toward your goal. This is the hard work of growing your wings: integrating new ideas to use with your spirited child when he's lost control again, taking a breath instead of shouting when you are *this close* to losing your patience with your toddler or teenager, not interrupting your husband when you're in the midst of a heated argument and it's his turn to talk. Your whole life offers you unexpected opportunities to work toward your goals.

Even your smallest efforts will get you through a door, which opens to a room full of windows of new opportunities you couldn't see before. Writes Martha Beck in *Finding Your Own North Star*: "Miracles really can and will occur when you connect with your dreams, but they're both more likely and less necessary if you do everything in your power to reach your goals."

Be curious. Bringing curiosity into your daily life is when you lean away from the predictability of your routine toward the sparkly unfamiliar opportunity that beckons.

Researchers Todd B. Kashdan and Paul J. Silvia define curiosity as "the recognition, pursuit, and intense desire to explore novel, challenging, and uncertain events…. Curiosity motivates people to act and think in new ways and investigate, be immersed, and learn about whatever is the immediate interesting target of their attention." Satisfying your curiosity can be as simple as ordering something new from your favorite take-out restaurant, asking questions to become acquainted with a new friend, or taking a new route to a familiar place.

Curiosity benefits you mentally, physically, and psychologically. Research studies show curiosity heightens well-being, improves your sense of self, lengthens your lifespan, reduces your risk of hypertension and diabetes, and helps your brain function better as you age. Out of the 24 character strengths identified by psychologists Martin Seligman and Christopher Peterson, curiosity is one of the five strengths strongly linked to overall happiness. (The other strengths correlated with happiness are hope, zest, gratitude, and love.)

Curiosity comes when you start listening to the voice of your essential self and begin to do new things that make your soul say, *More, please.* "Why not try following mere curiosity, with its humble, roundabout magic?" writes author Elizabeth Gilbert on oprah.com. "At the very least, it will keep you pleasantly distracted while life sorts itself out. At the very most, your curiosity may surprise you. Before you even realize what's happening, it may have led you safely all the way home."

What Pulls, What Shines

Monarch butterflies throughout Canada and the United States migrate to the same locations in California and Mexico each fall; large colonies of them fly long distances to places they've never been. How? The migrating monarchs have two built-in tools to get them to their safe locations where they weather out the winter: a type of magnetic compass in their brains that guides them toward their destination; and their antennas, which help them navigate by charting the path of the sun.

Just like a butterfly, you have everything you need to navigate toward a happy life. Knowing where to go is about trusting your essential self to continually guide you, like an inner magnet drawn to the rich ore of what feeds your soul. By using your essential self's attraction to what feels light, bright, and right, you can stay on the path to a life that continually enriches your soul.

Your happy place is as real as the trees the monarchs migrate to, a shelter where you're surrounded by a kaleidoscope of others like you.

Your journey may not be easy. You might believe that if you don't have your path mapped out yet, you probably won't–ever. Or, you might think that others possess an intuitive sense of how to follow the voice of their essential selves but this inner knowledge is missing in you. You may fear you'll always be lost.

But that's not the case. You will need to use courage, be curious, hold on to hope, and put in effort to get to that place where you belong, a place you've never been before.

When you do what fills you with expectant hope, insatiable curiosity, and sends an eager quiver of anticipation throughout your body, you'll find your way, following a path filled with what delights you and what is uniquely yours. If you don't yet know what that path is, be patient. "Just keep coming home to yourself," writes Byron Katie in *Loving What Is.* "You are the one you've been waiting for."

Practical Advice – Learned Optimism

When my husband and I are in the car and get lost or make a wrong turn, he asks, "What are we supposed to see here?" as if the problem is really an opportunity to discover something new. He's good that way–naturally able to look at the blessings hidden in the mistakes, the gifts buried beneath expectations of how things should be. It's not a Pollyanna affliction, but a lifelong skill that appeals to his hard-working heart. It's less about stumbling on the ruins and more about digging for the treasures in each moment.

Being optimistic has many benefits. Optimists are more successful because being optimistic helps you to achieve goals; you map out a plan and stick with it, even when it's difficult. Studies have shown that people who score higher on tests which measure optimistic thinking maintain greater levels of well-being and mental health during stressful periods. Optimists cope well when faced with challenges. They tend to be happier overall and physically healthier than pessimists, too.

"The defining characteristic of pessimists is that they tend to believe bad events will last a long time, will undermine everything they do, and are their own fault," writes Martin Seligman in *Learned Optimism: How to Change Your Mind and Your Life*. "The optimists, who are confronted with the same hard knocks of this world, think about misfortune in the opposite way. They tend to believe defeat is just a temporary setback, that its causes are confined to this one case. The optimists believe defeat is not their fault: Circumstances, bad luck, or other people brought it about. Such people are unfazed by defeat. Confronted by a bad situation, they perceive it as a challenge and try harder."

Optimism isn't a natural state for me. And if, like me, you find yourself on the glass-half-empty side of things, don't be discouraged—you can learn to become more optimistic by making choices to think differently about your circumstances. Here are some ways to do just that:

Visualize your future. Imagining the details of your best possible future and tuning in to your essential self for the details of what getting there would entail is a powerful exercise (as you will see in the Vision Board project at the end of this chapter). "The feeling you need is a desire, a genuine heartfelt longing, for something that lies right on the border between possibility and impossibility," writes Martha Beck in *Finding Your Own North Star*. Even if your vision seems unrealistic, far-fetched, or what Martha Beck calls *wildly improbable*, tuning in to what lights up your essential self allows you to use that brightness to illuminate the way toward getting what you desire, whether it's a shift in how you spend your free time, a change in where you live, or a revolution in your career that transforms your life and the lives of others.

Set goals and break them down into small steps. Once you listen to the voice of your essential self and imagine your ideal future, take a few of your far-fetched ideas and craft them into goals. Barbara Sher, author of *Wishcraft: How to Get What You Really Want*, emphasizes the need for goals to have a touchstone, what she defines as *"the emotional core of your goal*–what you want and need from it, what you love best about it."

Sher recommends using your touchstone to determine your first steps so that you can get the goodness from your goal right away, building excitement and momentum for more action. For example, if your goal is to sell your handmade jewelry on etsy.com and your touchstone is your desire to express your creativity on a regular basis, your motivational first step might be to start making jewelry right away, waiting to add the more practical business-building aspects until after your creative juices are flowing.

Try, try again. "You do your best work after your biggest disasters," said Broadway producer, director, and choreographer Jerome Robbins. When faced with disappointment, can you see it as an opportunity to learn, modify the plan, and try again? Instead of thinking that you're a failure when you find yourself yelling at your kids after resolving not to, use the situation as a way to develop more patience by identifying the many small incidences that led you to lose your temper. Look at your mistakes from the perspective of the Kind Caretaker–as lessons providing deep insights. "Failure creates an interesting tug of war between forgetting and remembering," writes dancer Twyla Tharp in *The Creative Habit: Learn it and Use it For Life*. "It's vital to be able to forget the pain of failure while retaining the lessons from it."

Acknowledge uncertainty. Sometimes you need to double check your optimism with a bit of perspective. "When facing an uncertain future, the rose-colored glasses of optimism serve us just fine," writes Paul Dolan in *Happiness by Design: Change What You Do, Not How You Think*, "as long as we can take them off from time to time for a dose of realism."

Motherhood is uncertain. It requires you to be hopeful for the best, but prepared for what might happen anyway–a temper tantrum with your three-year-old (or 13-year-old), a blown-out diaper, an unexpected phone call from the elementary school principal. Your joys are made sweeter by the salt of your experiences. The times when you struggle, the moments when you wish you could be anywhere but where you are, the days that fall apart with one failure after another, these are the experiences that sting, but they also create a density to the ocean of your motherhood: you are more buoyant, staying afloat, making your own way to shore.

Coaching + Craft – Creating Hope with a Vision Board

When you create a vision board, you sit your optimistic, dream-centered essential self at the crafting table with everything the essential self needs to imagine the future.

Creating a vision board is a simple project—you choose words and images from magazines and paste them on poster board—but its power is exceptional. When you collect pictures of what you want to be, do, create, experience, or have, you set intentions, clarify your unique desires, and allow an unfolding to occur. Research shows that the mind has the same reaction when visualizing an experience as it does when you actually have the experience.

When you create a vision board, you imagine *what* you want and don't focus at all on *how* it's going to happen. It's important to daydream during the vision board process so that you're in touch with your essential self. Once you have the images and the *what*, your social self can work with the essential self to notice opportunities, take action, and allow the *how* to happen.

Coaching + Craft Project Supplies

- Poster board, any size
- Magazines—ideally travel, art, home improvement, hobby, and lifestyle magazines. Collect a variety from friends and family or post on social networking sites like Freecycle, NextDoor Neighborhood, or craigslist to get additional magazines from your community.
- Scissors
- Glue. Repositional glue sticks work well with this project.

To begin, get in touch with your essential self by focusing on your breath, allowing yourself to notice what it is you want, not what's expected of you, not what you think others want from you, but what you truly want. Imagine that what you desire–whether it's an elusive feeling or a concrete goal–already belongs to you, then notice how this revelation feels in your body. Take a moment to notice and name the sensations you feel. This is your essential self, speaking to you through your body.

Use your body's responses as your guide to choose words and images for your vision board. Stay connected to your essential self as you go through magazines, cutting out pictures, words, and phrases that attract and interest you. Once you have a large pile, glue the images onto the poster board in a way that pleases your essential self.

When you're finished, hang your vision board in a visible place and take a photograph of it so you can refer to it when you're not home. Then use the vision board as your guide, allowing the process of stepping into your vision to unfold organically, noticing and taking advantage of opportunities that are aligned with the artistic inspiration you received from your essential self.

"It is said that all that you are seeking is also seeking you," writes author Clarissa Pinkola Estés. "If you lie still, sit still, it will find you. It has been waiting for you for a long time."

Choose this life, my friend. Not the one that might be waiting for you around the corner once your baby is sleeping through the night or your youngest child is in kindergarten–or middle school, or college. Not the life you loved before becoming a mother: childfree, carefree, but often missing the unexpected delight found in the unfolding of an ordinary day. Choose this life, with its tattered grace and transitory joys, and you'll give strength to the wings you've so carefully crafted. It's time to fly.

Endnotes

Introduction

Clarissa Pinkola Estés, *Women Who Run With the Wolves: Myths and Stories of the Wild Woman Archetype* (New York: Ballantine Books, 1996), 14.

Sara Beak, *Red, Hot and Holy: A Heretic's Love Story* (Boulder, Colorado: Sounds True, 2013), 128.

Peter Korn, *Why We Make Things and Why It Matters: The Education of a Craftsman* (New York: Random House, 2015), 7.

Barbara Kingsolver, as quoted in Mary Pipher, *Writing to Change the World* (New York: Penguin Group, 2006), 11.

Part 1 – REST

Anna Quindlen, *Being Perfect* (New York: Random House Publishing Group, 2009), 10.

Chapter One – Room

Pema Chodron, *When Things Fall Apart: Heart Advice for Difficult Times*, reprint (Boston: Shambhala Publications, 2005), 10.

Diane K. Osbon, editor, *A Joseph Campbell Companion: Reflections on the Art of Living* (New York: Harper Collins Publishers, Inc., 1991), 18.

Rebecca Dube, "Mom survey says: Three is the most stressful number of kids," Today Parents http://www.today.com/parents/mom-survey-says-three-most-stressful-number-kids-6C9774150

BabyCenter 21st Century Mom Insight Series: 2015 State of Modern
Motherhood Report, co-sponsored by Interactive Advertising
Bureau (San Francisco: February, 2015).

Louise L. Hay, *The Power is Within You* (Carlsbad, California: Hay
House, 1991), 7.

Chapter Two – Expect Less

Lev Grossman, *The Magician King* (New York: Plume, 2011).

Lisa Hammond Rashley, "Work it Out With Your Wife: Gendered
Expectations and Parenting Rhetoric Online," *NWSA Journal* 17:1
(Spring 2005): 58-92.

Susan G. Singley and Kathryn Hynes, "Transitions to Parenthood:
Work-Family Policies, Gender, and the Couple Context," *Gender
& Society* 17:3 (June 2005): 376-397.

Precilla Choi, Carole Henshaw, Sarah Baker, and J. Tree, "Supermum,
Superwife, Supereverything: Performing Femininity in the
Transition to Motherhood," *Journal of Reproductive and Infant
Psychology* 23:2 (May 2005):167-180.

Deborah Lupton, "A love/hate relationship: the ideals and experiences
of first-time mothers," *Journal of Sociology* 36:1 (March 2000): 50-
63.

Meghan Casserly, "ForbesWoman and TheBump.Com Survey Results,"
Forbes, http://www.forbes.com/sites/meghancasserly/2011/06/15/
forbeswoman-thebump-parentin-survey-results/

Wayne Dyer, "When you change the way you look at things, the
things you look at change," YouTube, https://www.youtube.com/
watch?v=urQPraeeY0w, April 19, 2008.

Carol McVeigh, "Motherhood Experiences from the Perspective of
First-Time Mothers," *Clinical Nursing Research* 6:4 (November
1997): 335-348.

Debra Kalmuss, Andrew Davidson and Linda Cushman, "Parenting Expectations, Experiences, and Adjustment to Parenthood: A Test of the Violated Expectations Framework," *Journal of Marriage and Family* 54:3 (August 1992): 516-526.

Holly Rust, "10 Times You Wish You Had a Mute Button for Your Toddler," Scary-Mommy, http://www.scarymommy.com/wish-mute-button-for-your-toddler/

Elizabeth Broadbent, "What I Wish I'd Known as a Newborn Mom," ScaryMommy, http://www.scarymommy.com/wish-id-known-newborn-mom/

Rebecca Dube, "Mom survey says: Three is the most stressful number of kids," Today Parents, http://www.today.com/parents/mom-survey-says-three-most-stressful-number-kids-6C9774150

Rakesh Sarin and Manel Baucells, *Engineering Happiness: A New Approach for Building a Joyful Life* (Berkeley, California: University of California Press, 2012), 49.

Byron Katie with Stephen Mitchell, *Loving What Is: Four Questions That Can Change Your Life* (New York: Three Rivers Press, 2002), 3.

J.K. Rowling, *Harry Potter and the Prisoner of Azkaban*, (New York: Scholastic Books, 1999), 238.

Karen Maezen Miller, *Momma Zen: Walking the Crooked Path of Motherhood* (Boston: Shambhala Publications, Inc., 2006), 16.

Sri Chinmoy, *The Wings of Joy: Finding Your Path to Inner Peace* (New York: Fireside, 1997), 163.

Brené Brown, *Daring Greatly: How the Courage to be Vulnerable Transforms the Way We Live, Love, Parent and Lead* (New York: Gotham Books, 2012), 195.

Thomas Gordon, *Parent Effectiveness Training: The Proven Program for Raising Responsible Children* (New York: Three Rivers Press, 2008), 127-130.

Mark Nepo, *The Exquisite Risk: Daring to Live an Authentic Life* (New York: Three Rivers Press, 2005), 218.

Meryl Streep, as quoted in Jena Pincott, *Mom Candy: 1,000 Quotes of Inspiration for Mothers* (New York: Random House, 2013), 182.

Chapter Three – Say No to the Book Fair

Mary Pipher, *Writing to Change the World* (New York: Riverhead Books, 2007), 95.

Melody Ross, The Brave Girls Club, http://bravegirlsclub.com/ (quote no longer online).

Rick Hanson, "Confronting the Negativity Bias," Rick Hanson, PhD: Resources for Happiness, Love, and Wisdom, https://www.rickhanson.net/how-your-brain-makes-you-easily-intimidated/

Clif Boutelle, "Women Find It More Difficult to Say 'No' to Excessive Workplace Requests," *Society for Industrial and Organizational Psychology*, http://www.siop.org/article_view.aspx?article=1336

Vanessa K. Bohns, M. Mahdi Roghanizad, and Amy Z. Xu, "Personality and Social Psychology Bulletin," *Personality and Social Psychology Bulletin* (December, 2013).

Brené Brown, "3 Ways to Set Boundaries: The importance of knowing when, and how, to say no," Oprah, http://www.oprah.com/spirit/How-to-Set-Boundaries-Brene-Browns-Advice

Vanessa M. Patrick and Henrik Hagtvedt, "'I Don't' versus 'I Can't': When Empowered Refusal Motivates Goal-Directed Behavior," Journal of Consumer Research 39:2 (August, 2012).

Boutelle, "Women Find It More Difficult to Say 'No' to Excessive Workplace Requests," http://www.siop.org/article_view.aspx?article=1336

Nancy Levin, *Jump...And Your Life Will Appear: An Inch-by-Inch Guide to Making a Major Change* (Carlsbad, California: Hay House, 2014).

Brown, "3 Ways to Set Boundaries: The importance of knowing when, and how, to say no," http://www.oprah.com/spirit/How-to-Set-Boundaries-Brene-Browns-Advice

Boutelle, "Women Find It More Difficult to Say 'No' to Excessive Workplace Requests," http://www.siop.org/article_view. aspx?article=1336

Dana R. Carney, Amy J.C. Cuddy, and Andy J. Yap, "Power Posing: Brief Nonverbal Displays Affect Neuroendocrine Levels and Risk Tolerance," *Psychological Science* 21:10 (October, 2010): 1363-1368.

Brown, http://www.oprah.com/spirit/How-to-Set-Boundaries-Brene-Browns-Advice

"DIY Tassel Key Chain Anthropologie Inspired," Kim Purvis, https://madeinaday.com/diy-tassel-key-chain-anthropologie-inspired/

Chapter Four – Take Your Time

Carlos Castaneda, *Journey To Ixtlan* (New York: Simon and Schuster, 2012), 184.

Laurie Tarkan, "Study: Working moms' stress levels linked to 'mental labor,'" Fox News, http://www.foxnews.com/health/2013/08/13/study-working-moms-stress-levels-linked-to-mental-labor

Shira Offer and Barbara Schneider, "Revisiting the Gender Gap in Time-Use Patterns: Multitasking and Well-Being Among Mothers and Fathers in Dual-Earner Families," *American Sociological Review* 76:6 (December, 2011): 809-833.

Earl Miller, quoted in Daniel J. Levitin, *The Organized Mind: Thinking Straight in the Age of Information Overload* (New York: Dutton, 2014), 169.

Alina Tugend, "Multitasking Can Make You Lose ... Um ... Focus," The New York Times, http://www.nytimes.com/2008/10/25/business/yourmoney/25shortcuts.html?pagewanted=all&_r=0

Chip Heath and Dan Health, *Switch: How to Change Things When Change is Hard* (New York: Crown Business, 2010), 131.

Theodore Roosevelt, as quoted on Goodreads, "Theodore Roosevelt: Quotes," https://www.goodreads.com/author/quotes/44567. Theodore_Roosevelt

Jonathan Haidt, *The Happiness Hypothesis: Finding Modern Truth in Ancient Wisdom* (New York: Basic Books, 2006), 26.

Jonathan Haidt, in Chip Heath and Dan Health, *Switch: How to Change Things When Change is Hard* (New York: Crown Business, 2010), 7-9.

Heath and Health, 7 and 19.

Michael Merzenich, as quoted by Anat Baniel, *Move Into Life: The Nine Essentials for Lifelong Vitality* (New York: Harmony Books, 2009), 176.

Martha Beck, "Turtle-Step Up! (And Up, And Up…)" Martha Beck: Creating Your Right Life, http://marthabeck.com/2010/07/turtle-step-up-and-up-and-up/

Marla Cilley, "FLYing Lesson: Declutter 15 Minutes a Day," FlyLady. net, http://www.flylady.net/d/getting-started/flying-lessons/decluttering-15-minutes/

Anat Baniel, *Move Into Life: The Nine Essentials for Lifelong Vitality* (New York: Harmony Books, 2009), 135-136.

"Project: Embellished Flip-Flops," Martha Stewart, http://www.marthastewart.com/268565/embellished-flip-flops

Part 2 – CRAFT

A.A. Milne, as quoted on Goodreads, "A.A. Milne: Quotes," https://www.goodreads.com/author/quotes/81466.A_A_Milne?page=2

Chapter Five – Carve Out Time for Yourself

Maria Edgeworth, as quoted on Goodreads, "Maria Edgeworth: Quotes," https://www.goodreads.com/author/quotes/82939. Maria_Edgeworth

Lane Strathearn, Jian Li, Peter Fonagy, and P. Read Montague, "What's in a Smile? Maternal Brain Responses to Infant Facial Cues," *Pediatrics* 122:1 (July, 2008): 40–51.

Johan N. Lundström, Annegret Mathe, Benoist Schaal, Johannes Frasnelli, Katharina Nitzsche, Johannes Gerber, and Thomas Hummel "Maternal status regulates cortical responses to the body odor of newborns," *Frontiers in Psychology* 4 (September 2013): 597.

James E. Swain, "Baby Stimuli and the Parent Brain: Functional Neuroimaging of the Neural Substrates of Parent-Infant Attachment," *Psychiatry* 5:8 (August, 2008): 28–36.

Andreas Bartels and Semir Zeki, "The neural correlates of maternal and romantic love," NeuroImage, 21 (2004): 1155–1166.

Pilyoung Kim, James F. Leckman, Linda C. Mayes, Ruth Feldman, Xin Wang, and James E. Swain, "The Plasticity of Human Maternal Brain: Longitudinal Changes in Brain Anatomy During the Early Postpartum Period," *Behavioral Neuroscience*, 124:5 (2010): 695–700.

Jennifer Barretta, Kathleen E. Woncha, Andrea Gonzalezb, Nida Alic, Meir Steinerb, Geoffrey B. Hallb, and Alison S. Fleming "Maternal affect and quality of parenting experiences are related to amygdala response to infant faces," *Social Neuroscience* 7:3 (September, 2012): 252-68.

Casserly, "ForbesWoman And TheBump.Com Survey Results," http://www.forbes.com/sites/meghancasserly/2011/06/15/forbeswoman-thebump-parentin-survey-results/

Suzanne Bianchi, John Robinson, and Melissa Milkie, *The Changing Rhythms of American Family Life* (New York: Russell Sage Foundation, 2007).

Regena Thomashauer, *Mama Gena's School of Womanly Arts* (New York: Simon & Schuster, 2003).

Rick Hanson, *Buddha's Brain: The Practical Neuroscience of Happiness, Love, and Wisdom* (Oakland, California: New Harbinger Publications, 2009).

Penelope Quest, *Reiki for Life: The Complete Guide to Reiki Practice for Levels 1, 2 & 3* (New York: Tarcher, 2010).

Miller, 165.

Chapter Six – Remember Why You Fell in Love

Mignon McLaughlin, *The Second Neurotic's Notebook* (Indianapolis, Indiana: Bobbs-Merrill Company, 1966).

Sonja Lyubomirsky, "Are Parents Happier or More Miserable? Usually Both. It Depends on the Type of Parent and Child," *Psychology Today*, https://www.psychologytoday.com/blog/how-happiness/201403/are-parents-happier-or-more-miserable

Jacqui Gabb, Martina Klett-Davies, Janet Fink, and Manuela Thomae, "Enduring Love? Couple Relationships in the 21st Century: Survey Findings," Economic and Social Research Council, (November, 2013), http://www.open.ac.uk/researchprojects/enduringlove/sites/www.open.ac.uk.researchprojects.enduringlove/files/files/Final-Enduring-Love-Survey-Report.pdf

John M. Gottman and Nan Silver, *The Seven Principles for Making Marriage Work: A Practical Guide from the Country's Foremost Relationship Expert* (New York: Three Rivers Press, 1999), 260-261.

Kathy Caprino, "What Selling 3 Million Copies Of 'The Dance Of Anger' Has Taught Renowned Psychologist Harriet Lerner," *Forbes*, http://www.forbes.com/sites/kathycaprino/2014/04/23/what-selling-3-million-copies-of-the-dance-of-anger-has-taught-renowned-psychologist-harriet-lerner/3/

Anna North, "Our Love Affair With Predicting Divorce," New York Times Opinion Pages, http://op-talk.blogs.nytimes.com/2014/07/11/our-love-affair-with-predicting-divorce/

The National Marriage Project's report, "2011 State of Our Unions: When Baby Makes Three: How Parenthood Makes Life Meaningful and How Marriage Makes Parenthood Bearable," University of Virginia, 2012.

W. Bradford Wilcox & Jeffrey Dew, "The Date Night Opportunity: What Does Couple Time Tell Us About the Potential Value of Date Nights?" The National Marriage Project at the University of Virginia, 2012.

Leo Tolstoy, as quoted on Goodreads, "Leo Tolstoy: Quotes," https://www.goodreads.com/author/quotes/128382.Leo_Tolstoy?page=2

Eli J. Finkel, Erica B. Slotter, Laura B. Luchies, Gregory M. Walton, and James J. Gross, "A Brief Intervention to Promote Conflict Reappraisal Preserves Marital Quality Over Time," *Psychological Science* 20:10 (June, 2013): 1-7.

Jeffrey Dew and W. Bradford Wilcox, "Generosity and the Maintenance of Marital Quality," *Journal of Marriage and Family* 75 (October 2013): 1218–1228.

Couples Training Institute, Gottman Couples & Marital Therapy: Background, http://couplestraininginstitute.com/gottman-couples-and-marital-therapy/

Flanagan, "The Last Marriage Post You'll Ever Need to Read," http://drkellyflanagan.com/2015/01/21/the-last-marriage-post-youll-ever-need-to-read/

James Wood, *Dictionary of Quotations from Ancient and Modern, English and Foreign Sources* (New York: Frederick Warne and Co., 1893), 11.

Thalita Murray, "DIY: A Pretty (& Easy) Dreamcatcher," Decoist, http://www.decoist.com/2015-03-18/diy-dreamcatcher-tutorial/

Mallory Jane, "Lace Dream Catcher," Hayseed Homemakin', http://www.hayseedhomemakin.com/2012/05/lace-dream-catcher.html

Chapter Seven – All about Guilt

Bill Watterson, *The Complete Calvin and Hobbes* (Riverside, New Jersey: Andrews McMeel Publishing, 2012).

Marybeth J. Mattingly and Suzanne M. Bianchi, "Gender Differences in the Quantity and Quality of Free Time: The U.S. Experience," *Social Forces* 81:3 (March, 2003): 999-1030.

The Working Mother Research Institute (WMRI), What Moms Choose: The Working Mother Report (New York, 2011).

"What Moms Choose: The Working Mother Report," Working Mother, http://www.workingmother.com/research-institute/what-moms-choose-working-mother-report

Evonne Lack, "Top 7 mommy guilt trips – and how to handle them," BabyCenter.com, http://www.babycenter.com/0_top-7-mommy-guilt-trips-8211-and-how-to-handle-them_3654967.bc?showAll=true

Katrina Alcorn, "Survey: 88% of Working Parents Suffer Stress-related Health Problems," Working Moms Break, http://www.workingmomsbreak.com/2011/06/20/survey-working-parents-health-problems/

Amy Ransom, "The Top 10 Things Mothers Feel Guilty About," Surviving Life and Motherhood (Just), http://www.amyransom.com/life-with-kids/guilt-mothers-prerogative

Kelly M. Flanagan, "Three Metaphors for the Outdated Institution of Marriage," Untangled, http://drkellyflanagan.com/2014/05/14/three-metaphors-for-the-outdated-institution-of-marriage/

Melissa A. Milkie, Kei M. Nomaguchi, and Kathleen E. Denny, "Does the Amount of Time Mothers Spend With Children or Adolescents Matter?" *Journal of Marriage and Family* 77 (April, 2015): 355–372.

Rachel G. Lucas-Thompson, Wendy A. Goldberg, and JoAnn Prause, "Maternal Work Early in the Lives of Children and Its Distal

Associations with Achievement and Behavior Problems: A Meta-Analysis," *Psychological Bulletin* 136:6 (2010): 915–942.

Jena McGregor, "The Potential Payoff for Kids of Working Mothers," The Washington Post, http://www.washingtonpost.com/blogs/on-leadership/wp/2015/05/19/the-potential-payoff-for-kids-of-working-mothers/

Carmen Nobel, "Children Benefit From Having a Working Mom," Harvard Business School, http://www.hbs.edu/news/articles/Pages/mcginn-working-mom.aspx

Brené Brown, *The Gifts of Imperfection: Let Go of Who You Think You're Supposed to Be and Embrace Who You Are* (Center City, Minnesota: Hazelden, 2010), 23.

Roy F. Baumeister, Arlene M. Stillwell, and Todd F. Heatherton, "Guilt: An Interpersonal Approach" *Psychological Bulletin* 115: 2 (1994): 243-26.

Ransom, "The Top 10 Things Mothers Feel Guilty About," http://www.amyransom.com/life-with-kids/guilt-mothers-prerogative

Bob McLeod, *Superhero ABC* (New York: HarperCollins, 2006).

Daniel Y. Kimberg, Mark D'Esposito, and Martha J. Farah, "Cognitive Functions in the Prefrontal Cortex: Working Memory and Executive Control," *Current Directions in Psychological Science* 6:6 (December, 1997): 185-192.

Seung-Schik Yoo, Ninad Gujar, Peter Hu, Ferenc A. Jolesz, and Matthew P. Walker, "The Human Emotional Brain Without Sleep: A Prefrontal Amygdala Disconnect," *Current Biology* 17:20 (October, 2007): R877–R878.

Kelly McGonigal, *The Willpower Instinct: How Self-Control Works, Why It Matters, and What You Can Do To Get More of It* (New York: Avery, 2011), 62.

BJ Gallagher,"Why Don't We Do The Things We Know Are Good For Us?" HuffPost Healthy Living, http://www.huffingtonpost.com/ bj-gallagher/why-dont-we-do-the-things_b_409428.html

Lyubomirsky, *The How of Happiness*, 112.

Chapter Eight – Find Friends

Jane Howard, *Families* (Piscataway, New Jersey: Transaction Publishers, 1998), 234.

Ashley McGuire, "Millennial Motherhood: Connected But Lonely," Family Studies, http://family-studies.org/millennial-motherhood-connected-but-lonely/

Rachel Bertsche, *MWF Seeking BFF: My Yearlong Search for a New Best Friend* (New York: Ballantine Books, 2011), 6.

Simone Schnall, Kent D. Harber, Jeanine K. Stefanucci, and Dennis R. Proffitt, "Social Support and the Perception of Geographical Slant," *Journal of Experimental Social Psychology* 44:5 (September, 2008): 1246–1255.

Tom Rath, Vital Friends: The People You Can't Afford To Live Without (New York: Gallup Press, 2006), 24.

Julianne Holt-Lunstad, Timothy B. Smith, J. Bradley Layton, "Social Relationships and Mortality Risk: A Meta-analytic Review," PLOS Medicine (July, 2010).

Rath, 9-10.

Rath, 9-10.

Jennifer Robison, "Happiness is Love -- and $75,000," Business Journal, http://www.gallup.com/businessjournal/150671/ happiness-is-love-and-75k.aspx

Rath, 9-10.

Bertsche, 203.

Holt-Lunstad, Smith, and Layton.

Miller McPherson, Lynn Smith-Lovin, and Matthew E. Brashears, "Social Isolation in America: Changes in Core Discussion Networks over Two Decades," *American Sociological Review* 71:3 (June 2006): 353-375

Holt-Lunstad, Smith, and Layton.

Bertsche, 206.

Shelley E. Taylor, Laura Cousino Klein, Brian P. Lewis, Tara L. Gruenewald, Regan A. R. Gurung, and John A. Updegraff, "Biobehavioral Responses to Stress in Females: Tend-and-Befriend, Not Fight-or-Flight," *Psychological Review* 107:3 (2000): 411.

Anne Lamott, *Stitches: A Handbook on Meaning, Hope and Repair* (New York: Riverhead Books, 2013).

Bertsche, 81.

Brown, *Daring Greatly*, 41.

Lois M. Verbrugge, "Multiplexity in Adult Friendships," Social Forces 57:4 (1979): 1286-1309.

Paramahansa Yogananda, as quoted on Goodreads, "Paramahansa Yogananda: Quotes," https://www.goodreads.com/author/quotes/14650.Paramahansa_Yogananda

Chapter Nine – Talk Nicely

David James Lees, "The Tao of Self-Talk (Part 2)," David James Lees: Wu Wei Wisdom, https://davidjameslees.wordpress.com/2012/08/24/the-tao-of-self-talk-part-2/

Brown, *The Gifts of Imperfection*, 38.

Tara Brach, *Radical Authenticity: Embracing Your Life with the Heart of a Buddha* (New York: Bantam Books, 2003), 3.

Joanne V. Wood, W.Q. Elaine Perunovic, and John W. Lee "Positive Thinking: Power for Some, Peril for Others," *Psychological Science* 20:7 (2009): 860-866.

Hanson, "Confronting the Negativity Bias," https://www.rickhanson.net/how-your-brain-makes-you-easily-intimidated/

Hanson, "Confronting the Negativity Bias," https://www.rickhanson.net/how-your-brain-makes-you-easily-intimidated/

Tami Simon and Kristin Neff, "Session 1: Compassion for the Self-Critic," *The Self-Acceptance Project*, http://live.soundstrue.com/selfacceptance/event.php

Martha Beck, *Steering by Starlight: The Science and Magic of Finding your Destiny* (New York: Rodale, 2009), 35.

Allison C. Kelly, David C. Zuroff, and Leah B. Shapira, "Soothing Oneself and Resisting Self-Attacks: The Treatment of Two Intrapersonal Deficits in Depression Vulnerability," Cognitive Therapy and Research 33 (2009): 301–313.

Brown, *Daring Greatly*, 66.

Martha Beck, "How to Tune Into Your Inner Wisdom," *Martha Beck: Creating Your Right Life*, http://marthabeck.com/2013/10/inner-wisdom/

Russ Harris, *ACT with Love: Stop Struggling, Reconcile Differences, and Strengthen Your Relationship with Acceptance and Commitment Therapy* (Oakland, California: New Harbinger Publications, 2009), 177-178.

Tara Parker-Pope, "Go Easy on Yourself, a New Wave of Research Urges," *The New York Times*, http://well.blogs.nytimes.com/2011/02/28/go-easy-on-yourself-a-new-wave-of-research-urges/

Janet Polivy and C. Peter Herman as quoted in Kelly McGonigal, *The Willpower Instinct: How Self-Control Works, Why It Matters, and What You Can Do to Get More of It* (New York: Penguin, 2011), 144.

Kelly McGonigal, "Is There Such a Thing as "Shame" Power? Why shame can both help and Hurt Self-Control," *Psychology Today*, https://www.psychologytoday.com/blog/the-science-willpower/201112/is-there-such-thing-shame-power

McGonigal, *The Willpower Instinct*, 145.

Kristin D. Neff and Christopher K. Germer, "A Pilot Study and Randomized Controlled Trial of the Mindful Self-Compassion Program," *Journal of Clinical Psychology* (2012): 1-17.

Kristin D. Neff and Andrew P. Costigan, "Self-Compassion, Wellbeing, and Happiness," *Psychologie in Österreich* 2:3 (2014): 114-119.

Stephanie S. Rude, Kacey Little Maestas, and Kristin Neff, "Paying Attention to Distress: What's Wrong with Rumination?" *Cognition and Emotion* 21:4 (2007): 843-864.

Christopher K. Germer, T*he Mindful Path to Self-Compassion: Freeing Yourself from Destructive Thoughts and Emotions* (New York: Guilford Press, 2009), 2.

Lamott, *Stitches*, 63.

Lyubomirsky, *The How of Happiness*, 129-130.

Lyubomirsky, *The How of Happiness*, 127-129.

Lyubomirsky, *The How of Happiness*, 133.

Lyubomirsky, *The How of Happiness*, 133.

Amelia Earhart, quoted in Amelia Earhart: The Official Website, http://www.ameliaearhart.com/about/quotes.html

A.A. Milne, quoted in Goodreads, "A.A. Milne: Quotes," https://www.goodreads.com/author/quotes/81466.A_A_Milne

Amanda Formaro, "Painted Rock Garden Markers," Crafts by Amanda, http://craftsbyamanda.com/painted-rock-garden-markers/

Part 3 – FLY

Amy Tiemann, quoted in Amy Tiemann: Courage to Lead, Power to Change, "Amy Tiemann: Quotes," http://amytiemann.com/quotes/

Chapter Ten – Find Fun

Elizabeth Gilbert, *Eat, Pray, Love: One Woman's Search for Everything Across Italy, India and Indonesia* (New York: Penguin, 2006), 115.

Mihaly Csikszentmihalyi, *Finding Flow: The Psychology of Engagement with Everyday Life* (New York: Basic Books, 1997), 65.

Csikszentmihalyi, *Finding Flow*, 75.

Anat Baniel, *Move Into Life: The Nine Essentials for Lifelong Vitality* (New York: Harmony Books, 2009), 165.

Baniel, 167.

Stuart Brown, M.D., *Play: How It Shapes the Brain, Opens the Imagination, and Invigorates the Soul* (New York: Penguin Group, 2009), 17-18.

Leon Neyfakh, "What playfulness can do for you: Research discovers the many benefits of being a goofball," *The Boston Globe*, http://www.bostonglobe.com/ideas/2014/07/19/what-playfulness-can-for-you/Cxd7Et4igTLkwpkUXSr3cO/story.html

Brown, *Play*, 152-153.

Brown, *Play*, 212.

Amit Kumar, Matthew A. Killingsworth, and Thomas Gilovich, "Waiting for Merlot: Anticipatory Consumption of Experiential and Material Purchases," *Psychological Science* 25:10 (October, 2014): 1924-1931.

Leaf Van Boven and Thomas Gilovich, "To Do or To Have? That is the Question," *Journal of Personality and Social Psychology* 85:6 (2003): 1193–1202.

Mihaly Csikszentmihalyi, "Flow: The Psychology of Optimal Experience," Global Learning Communities, 2000, 2-3.

Csikszentmihalyi, *Finding Flow*, 66.

Martin E. P. Seligman, *Flourish: A Visionary New Understanding of Happiness and Well-Being* (New York: Simon and Schuster, 2012), 16.

Csikszentmihalyi, "Flow: The Psychology of Optimal Experience," 3.

Brown, *Play*, 127.

Brown, *Play*, 144.

Paul Dolan, *Happiness by Design: Change What You Do Not How You Think* (New York: Hudson Street Press, 2014), 147-148.

Brown, *Play*, 133-134.

Csikszentmihalyi, *Finding Flow*, 77.

Brown, *Play*, 11.

Brown, *Play*, 11-12.

Tijana Popovic, "Money Saving Monday: Table Decor," Frugal Living Adventures, https://frugallivingadventures.wordpress.com/tag/stir-stick/

Chapter Eleven – Live by Heart

Martha Beck, "The 5-Step Plan to Set Your Heart Free," Oprah, http://www.oprah.com/spirit/Martha-Becks-Plan-to-Get-Unstuck-and-Follow-Your-Dreams

Annie O'Shaughnessy, "Deep Healing through Truth Telling," True Nature Guidance, http://truenatureguidance.blogspot.com/2014/03/deep-healing-through-truth-telling.html

Brown, *The Gifts of Imperfection*, 49.

Martha Beck, "Cry Freedom! Insight from Martha," Martha Beck: Creating Your Right Life, http://marthabeck.com/2011/06/cry-freedom-insight-from-martha/

Brown, *The Gifts of Imperfection*, 50.

Martha Beck, *Finding Your Own North Star: Claiming the Life You Were Meant To Live* (New York: MJF Books, 2001), 4.

Martha Beck, Facebook post, https://www.facebook.com/marthabeckauthor/posts/531183306970847

Roxanne Hai, "Being vulnerable about vulnerability: Q&A with Brené Brown," TED Blog, http://blog.ted.com/being-vulnerable-about-vulnerability-qa-with-brene-brown/

C.G. Jung, *The Archetypes and the Collective Unconscious: Collected Works of C.G. Jung*, revised (London: Routledge, 2014), 384.

Jon Kabat-Zinn, as quoted in Dena Rosenbloom and Mary Beth Williams, *Life After Trauma, Second Edition: A Workbook for Healing* (New York: Guilford Publications, 2010), 39-40.

C. G. Jung, *The Essential Jung: Selected and Introduced by Anthony Storr*, revised (Princeton, New Jersey: Princeton University Press, 2013), 234.

"C.G. Jung: 'The mandala is… the path to the center, to individuation,'" Jung Currents, http://jungcurrents.com/jung-individuation-mandala

Natasha Linton, "DIY Dishwasher Safe Decorating Plates and Mugs – Sharpies, Sharpie Pens, and Alcohol Inks," The Artisan Life, http://www.natashalh.com/diy-dishwasher-safe-decorating-plates-and-mugs-sharpies-sharpie-pens-and-alcohol-inks/

Renee Zarate, "A Gratitude Mandala for Craft Stamper November Challenge," Bolton House, http://renee-boltonhouse.blogspot.com/2014/11/a-gratitude-mandala-for-craft-stamper_14.html?m=1

Chapter Twelve – Your Turn

Maulana Jalal al-Din Rumi, as quoted on Goodreads, "Rumi: Quotes," https://www.goodreads.com/author/quotes/875661.Rumi

Alan Cohen, *A Deep Breath of Life: Daily Inspiration for Heart-Centered Living* (Carlsbad, California: Hay House, 1996), 4.

Eleanor Roosevelt, *You Learn by Living*, revised (Louisville, Kentucky: Westminster John Knox Press, 1960), 41.

Salvatore R. Maddi, "Hardiness: The courage to grow from stresses," *The Journal of Positive Psychology* 1:3 (July, 2006): 160-168.

Mary Ann Radmacher, quoted in Nina Lesowitz and Mary Beth Sammons, *The Courage Companion: How to Live Life with True Power* (Berkeley, California: Cleis Press, 2010), 11.

Jeff Grabmeier, "You've Got To Have Hope: Studies Show 'Hope Therapy' Fights Depression," Research News, http://researchnews.osu.edu/archive/apahope.htm

Robert Weis and Elena C Speridakos, "A Meta-Analysis of Hope
    Enhancement Strategies in Clinical and Community Settings,"
    Psychology of Well-Being: Theory, Research and Practice 1:5
    (November, 2011): http://www.psywb.com/content/1/1/5

Anthony Scioli and Henry B. Biller, *Hope in the Age of Anxiety: A Guide
    to Understanding and Strengthening Our Most Important Virtue*
    (New York: Oxford University Press, 2009), 341.

Katie with Mitchell, *Loving What Is*, 23.

Anne Lamott, as quoted in Anthony Scioli and Henry B. Biller, *Hope in the
    Age of Anxiety: A Guide to Understanding and Strengthening Our Most
    Important Virtue* (New York: Oxford University Press, 2009), 210.

Marina Krakovsky, "The Effort Effect," Stanford Alumni, https://
    alumni.stanford.edu/get/page/magazine/article/?article_id=32124

Beck, *Finding Your Own North Star*, 306.

Todd B. Kashdan and Paul J. Silvia, "Curiosity and Interest: The
    Benefits of Thriving on Novelty and Challenge," in C. R. Snyder
    and Shane J. Lopez, ed., *Oxford Handbook of Positive Psychology*
    (New York: Oxford University Press, 2009), 368.

Todd B. Kashdan and Michael F. Steger, "Curiosity and Pathways
    to Well-Being and Meaning in Life: Traits, States, and Everyday
    Behaviors," *Motivation and Emotion* 31 (September, 2007): 159–173

Todd B. Kashdan, Paul Rose, and Frank D. Fincham, "Curiosity
    and Exploration: Facilitating Positive Subjective Experiences and
    Personal Growth Opportunities," *Journal of Personality Assessment*
    82:3 (2004): 291-305.

Todd Kasdan, "The Power of Curiosity," Experience Life, https://
    experiencelife.com/article/the-power-of-curiosity/

Elizabeth Gilbert, "What to Do if You Can't Find Your Passion,"
    Oprah, http://www.oprah.com/spirit/Elizabeth-Gilbert-on-the-
    Importance-of-Curiosity

Hadley Leggett, "Butterflies Use Antenna GPS to Guide Migration," *Wired*, http://www.wired.com/2009/09/monarch-migration/

Christine Merlin, Robert J. Gegear, and Steven M. Reppert, "Antennal Circadian Clocks Coordinate Sun Compass Orientation in Migratory Monarch Butterflies," *Science* 325:5948 (September, 2009): 1700-1704.

Hoai-Tran Bui, "Monarch butterflies use magnetic compass to migrate," USA Today, http://www.usatoday.com/story/news/nation/2014/06/24/monarch-butterflies-migration-patterns-research-steven-reppert/11267655/

Katie with Mitchell, *Loving What Is*, 312.

Ciro Conversano, Alessandro Rotondo, Elena Lensi, Olivia Della Vista, Francesca Ar-pone, and Mario Antonio Reda, "Optimism and Its Impact on Mental and Physical Well-Being," *Clinical Practice Epidemiology and Mental Health* 6 (May, 2010): 25–29.

"Mindfulness and Positive Thinking: Optimism," The Pursuit of Happiness, http://www.pursuit-of-happiness.org/science-of-happiness/positive-thinking/

Sara Rimer and Madeline Drexler, "Happiness & Health," Harvard School of Public Health, http://www.hsph.harvard.edu/news/magazine/happiness-stress-heart-disease/

Martin Seligman, *Learned Optimism: How to Change Your Mind and Your Life* (New York: Knopf Doubleday Publishing Group, 2011), 4.

Beck, *Finding Your Own North Star*, 304.

Barbara Sher, *Wishcraft: How to Get What You Really Want* (New York: Ballantine Books, 1979), 66.

Jerome Robbins, quoted in Twyla Tharp, *The Creative Habit: Learn It and Use It For Life* (New York: Simon & Schuster, 2003), 214.

Twyla Tharp, *The Creative Habit: Learn It and Use It For Life* (New York: Simon & Schuster, 2003), 214.

Dolan, 97.

Clarissa Pinkola Estés, *Women Who Run with the Wolves: Myths and Stories of the Wild Woman Archetype* (New York: Ballantine Books, 1992), 152.

Acknowledgments

This book would not be what it is without the gentle force that is Grace Kerina. As my editor, she provided a steady wind that kept my ideas, words, and phrases moving toward the welcome shore of my final manuscript.

I'm grateful for the team at Morgan James Publishing, especially David Hancock and Bonnie Rausch, who patiently guided me step-by-step through the process of launching *The Well-Crafted Mom* into the world.

Thank you to photographer (and brother-in-law) Christopher White of littlebluemarblegallery.com for my author photo.

I am so grateful to Kristy Camacho, who read early versions of this book, patiently fielded all sorts of questions, and helped to shape the book by sharing her wisdom, steadfast support, and ability to see the bright side of everything. I am thankful for my other early readers: Stacie Gregori and Aubri Tallent. As mothers of small children, they dedicated rare free time to read my manuscript and provide feedback. Thank you to these three Well-Crafted Moms for sharing their knowledge, insight, and experience; my book is better for it.

Thank you to my coaching clients and to the moms who joined my Coaching + Craft gatherings each month. I've learned so much from each of you.

My dance instructors, Cheryl Ringman and Patti Stetson Michelsen, and Tai Chi teacher, Elliotte Mao, helped me move my way back into my body after hours and hours of sitting at my computer. Thank you for giving me tools to ease my stress.

I'm grateful for my beloved friends in The Coaches Guild for all their love and support: Eleni Cardona, Lisa Kuzman, Deborah Hodson, Gianna Brasil, Ann Kates, Jennifer Wayne, Paula Sladek LeGros, and Christy Miller. Our retreat fell smack dab in the middle of crucial writing deadlines, but I wouldn't have missed our weekend for the world. My creative spark was nurtured by all of you and in the quiet early-morning hours I spent writing in Deborah's home, a haven in the hills.

For the women who helped me set my sails: Annie O'Shaughnessy, for the retreat where I started shedding my second skin; Melody Ross and Kathy Wilkins of the Brave Girls Club, for the strength and insight I gained through their programs; and Martha Beck, for her inspiration, tools, and training that provided me with a solid foundation to do my best work.

Thank you to the wise and wonderful Sally Hayman, LCSW, for helping my husband and me reweave the loose threads of our marriage.

And thank you to family and friends for their support: Barbara and Douglas Harper, Julia Cooper, Sally and Michael Harper, Laura Harper and Jenn Wright, Valerie and William Harper, Tom Harper, Pamela and Ted Truscott, Christopher White, my many nieces and nephews, and my friends Kathryn O'Brien, Stefanie Soe Benson, Janice Nelson, Eliana Armstrong, Deborah Hecht, Samantha Mar, Reta Coolin, and Deborah Graves.

Thank you to the indomitable Christy Miller of Point Be Coaching—friend, life coach, and guide—for ever-so-nicely kicking me in the pants when I needed to sit my butt back down in the chair and finish the book. I am eternally grateful for your friendship, wise counsel, and bottomless love.

Thank you to my two sons. You are my greatest gifts and wisest teachers. I love you more than you will ever know (until you grow up and have children of your own).

I'm forever grateful to my husband, William White, the most patient, supportive, and loving man I know. The love, faith, and magic we share is the updraft that allows me to soar.

Thank You

Thank you so much for reading *The Well-Crafted Mom*.

To continue the journey we started together in the pages of this book, I've created two Coaching + Craft videos with new topics and crafts to give you extra support. In these videos, you'll get step-by-step tutorials for creating two crafts as well as additional self-coaching tools and resources for handling situations where moms frequently have trouble and need a little help.

Video #1: How Will You Spend Your Day?

Imagine that each morning you get a handful of golden coins to put in your pocket. These coins represent how much energy–emotional, physical, and spiritual–is available for you to spend throughout the day. The amount of coins you get varies from zero to ten each day, depending on many factors, like quality and quantity of sleep, stress level, and how many commitments, obligations, and responsibilities are tugging at you, trying to get your attention.

How do you know how many coins you have to spend for the day and how do you decide where to spend them?

Watch this video to learn how to use this self-coaching tool to better manage your days. In the Coaching + Craft tutorial, you'll follow easy steps for decorating a small dish that will remind you to decide each morning how you'll spend your day.

Video #2: Re-Pairing Your Relationship

"A successful marriage requires falling in love many times, always with the same person," wrote author Mignon McLaughlin. And it's true. As your relationship changes over time, with the addition of children and stressors that come from within and outside of your partnership, your marriage must change, too. The challenge, says Esther Perel, author of *Mating in Captivity and The State of Affairs*, is to not only repair your relationship but to *re-pair* it–renegotiating and redefining the partnership.

In this video, I'll share ideas on how to re-pair your partnership so it's more resilient and offer suggestions on how you can reconnect with your spouse. In the Coaching + Craft tutorial you'll learn how to create a bracelet using recycled buttons, a pretty reminder that the ordinary and familiar can be transformed into something that feels delightful and new.

Visit thewellcraftedmom.com/book-thanks to download your free videos. And, while you're there, check out the mommy mentoring work I do, including one-on-one life coaching, presentations, and retreats for moms.

Big hugs!
Kathleen Ann Harper

Contact Information
Website: thewellcraftedmom.com
Facebook: facebook.com/thewellcraftedmom
Instagram: instagram.com/thewellcraftedmom
Twitter: twitter.com/wellcraftedmom

About the Author

Kathleen Ann Harper is an eager reader, enthusiastic tap dancer, and avid crafter. She's the co-author of *Signs of a Happy Baby: The Baby Sign Language Book*, which she wrote with her husband, William Paul White. A certified life coach for moms, Kathleen is passionate about sharing smart self-care solutions for managing motherhood through her writing, life coaching, presentations, and retreats. She holds a Bachelor of Arts degree in Integrative Healing, which incorporated coursework in psychology, philosophy and religion, holistic health, and kinesiology. Kathleen lives in San Mateo, California, with her husband, two teenaged sons, a rambunctious poodle that makes Kathleen laugh every day, and a beloved tabby cat that rolls over and fetches.

Morgan James
Speakers Group

www.TheMorganJamesSpeakersGroup.com

We connect Morgan James published authors with live and online events and audiences who will benefit from their expertise.